An
Unknown
World

For Eliza and Eric —

With a great wish for
your own inner search

Jacob Needleman

JEREMY P. TARCHER/PENGUIN
a member of Penguin Group (USA) Inc.
New York

An Unknown World

Notes on the Meaning of the Earth

JACOB NEEDLEMAN

JEREMY P. TARCHER/PENGUIN
Published by the Penguin Group
Penguin Group (USA) Inc., 375 Hudson Street, New York, New York
10014, USA • Penguin Group (Canada), 90 Eglinton Avenue East, Suite 700, Toronto,
Ontario M4P 2Y3, Canada (a division of Pearson Penguin Canada Inc.) • Penguin Books Ltd,
80 Strand, London WC2R 0RL, England • Penguin Ireland, 25 St Stephen's Green,
Dublin 2, Ireland (a division of Penguin Books Ltd) • Penguin Group (Australia),
250 Camberwell Road, Camberwell, Victoria 3124, Australia (a division of Pearson Australia
Group Pty Ltd) • Penguin Books India Pvt Ltd, 11 Community Centre, Panchsheel Park,
New Delhi–110 017, India • Penguin Group (NZ), 67 Apollo Drive, Rosedale, North Shore 0632,
New Zealand (a division of Pearson New Zealand Ltd) • Penguin Books
(South Africa) (Pty) Ltd, 24 Sturdee Avenue, Rosebank, Johannesburg 2196, South Africa

Penguin Books Ltd, Registered Offices: 80 Strand, London WC2R 0RL, England

Grateful acknowledgment is made to reprint the following:
Excerpts from *In Search of the Miraculous* by P. D. Ouspensky. Copyright 1949 by Houghton Mifflin
Harcourt Publishing Company. Copyright © renewed 1977 by Tatiana Nagro. Reprinted by permission
of Houghton Mifflin Harcourt Publishing Company. All rights reserved.

Most Tarcher/Penguin books are available at special quantity discounts for bulk purchase
for sales promotions, premiums, fund-raising, and educational needs. Special books
or book excerpts also can be created to fit specific needs. For details, write Penguin
Group (USA) Inc. Special Markets, 375 Hudson Street, New York, NY 10014.

Library of Congress Cataloging-in-Publication Data
Needleman, Jacob.
An unknown world : notes on the meaning of the earth / Jacob Needleman.
p.   cm.
Includes bibliographical reference and index.
ISBN 978-1-58542-901-1
1. Earth—Philosophy. I. Title.
QB631.N44   2012   2012023955
113—dc23

Printed in the United States of America
1   3   5   7   9   10   8   6   4   2

BOOK DESIGN BY NICOLE LAROCHE

ALWAYS LEARNING   PEARSON

For My Companions

Acknowledgments

I wish to express my gratitude to the Mesa Refuge in Point Reyes Station, California, for an especially fruitful writing retreat during the summer of 2010. There, near to the Pacific Ocean and amid the rhythms of the tidal wetlands and the all-embracing green life, this book quietly carried itself forward from its very first beginnings.

Much thanks also to Charles H. Langmuir, professor of geochemistry, Harvard University, for access to the then-unpublished revised edition of *How to Build a Habitable Planet: The Story of Earth from the Big Bang to Humankind,* co-authored with Wally Broecker, which masterfully places the question of the fate of the Earth within the vast scientific narrative of the evolving universe as our planet now either ascends or descends through human hands.

Once again, but this time even more poignantly, I am deeply grateful to my editor, Mitch Horowitz, for the kind of support that every author dreams of.

And I owe very, very much to those friends and companions who read or heard parts of this book in the making and who emanated a degree of goodwill that made me feel the wind rise at my back whenever I most needed it.

And to my wife, Gail? Everything.

Contents

An
Unknown
World

Chapter One

The Low Stone Wall

A month ago, on the night of my seventy-fifth birthday, I dreamed of Elias Barkhordian. I was once again sitting on the low stone wall surrounding our neighbor's lawn, where Elias and I would always go to talk about the universe. As it had been then, over sixty years ago, so it was in the dream: late afternoon in October, the sun low in the sky; in the distance the shouts of the neighborhood children at their street games. And, as it also was then, I had been walking away from the noise, pretending to be walking aimlessly, but knowing I would be meeting Elias. And as for Elias, who soon appeared from across Seventh Street where the rich people lived, he was also pretending to be just walking, and when we met we pretended to be a little surprised—that was our ritual, played out for several years until Elias died just before his fourteenth birthday.

As we walked toward each other in the dream, I could not see him clearly; I especially could not make out his face. It was only when we sat down on the stone wall that I really was able to see him. He was as I remembered him: his big, heavy body, his large moon face; shining black hair and shining pitch-black eyes under a serene, wide forehead.

I started to talk to him, not really surprised to see him alive. I was saying something about God and the stars and the planets, about life and death and the mind—our usual topics. He said nothing, but when I uttered the word "death," he started aging before my eyes. I kept on talking— in the dream my words made no sound—as I watched him grow older, his forehead crowding with crisscrossing lines, his eyes glowing more and more brightly. I started to feel deep grief; I thought my heart would burst, and in my sleep I could sense my chest heaving.

"Elias!" I shouted noiselessly in the dream, "Elias! What should we do? What should we do?"

He was now as old as he would have been had he still been alive. He said nothing.

Suddenly, he looked at me with a mixture of sorrow and disappointment.

I woke up. My face was wet with tears.

I COULD NOT let go of that dream. During the whole of that day I tried to recollect times the two of us had spent sitting on the stone wall—even when it was covered with ice, or while snow was falling. When it was raining heavily, however, we would go to the big house he lived in, where his beautiful Armenian mother would serve us delicious cakes and strangely fragrant tea.

During the day after the dream, I went through my library and looked for any books that I still had from that period of my early life, in order to freshen my memories of my childhood friend. It was then that I knew I had to try to write about the Earth, something that for a long time I had resisted.

Surely there is no more urgent problem facing our world than our relation to the Earth. But over the years each time I turned this subject over in my mind I could not find the one great idea that would justify any attempt that I could make to add to the vast literature that now exists and continues to grow about the future of the Earth. No other question, no other crisis, has called to so many different voices, so many realms of thought and feeling, so many minds, with so many agendas and purposes, so many interconnections in economics, education, politics, philosophy,

sociology, art, religion, medicine, engineering, agricul-
ture—not to mention, of course, in the sciences of paleontology, meteorology, biology, geology, geochemistry and
many others. And also: Within and above this great question stand the needs of the oppressed or downtrodden
peoples of developing nations, the crisis of world poverty,
the crisis of energy, the agendas of corporations, the planetary depredations of vast criminal forces, the call to far-
reaching social activism, the ominous facts of pollution
and world population, the accelerating crisis of water . . .

. . . and on and on. Each of these elements offers or cries
out for its own answer, its own solution, its own understanding. Behind each stand great bodies of research, expertise, argument, history, wars past, present and future.

And in any case, in all of this there was certainly no
need for one more book of the kind that I could offer.

All that changed the day following my dream.

Chapter Two

What Is a World?

I spent hours in my attic opening dusty cartons of old books. I was especially hoping to find a particular book that had made a great impression on me when I was young: *The Mysterious Universe*, by the astronomer and mathematician Sir James Jeans.

I felt it would help me remember my friend Elias and some of our conversations. But I came across nothing that dated that far back—over sixty years—in my life.

Then all at once my heart leaped.

Could it be?

It was an oversized book, its gray faded cover damaged by mold, its spine hanging by a few threads. The moment I touched it, I knew what it was: *The Stars for Sam*. It was like looking for silver and finding gold.

I remained sitting cross-legged on the floor. For a long
moment I simply held the book. So much of me was in the
pages of that book that I was almost afraid to open it. My
childhood love of astronomy was in it. And my childhood
love of astronomy had been the seed of my wish for truth
and my sense of wonder in front of the vastness of the universe and the wholeness and the livingness of reality. The
author of the book had written it for older children and
had succeeded, at least for me, in evoking a sense of the
sacred. Such books, having this kind of action on the mind
of a young person, are rare and are desperately needed.

The first title page bore the inscription "To Jerry From
Mother, 4/23/43." I was then eight years old.

I began turning the pages, pausing in front of the
quaintly illustrated first letters of each chapter, looking at
scientific diagrams and photographs long superseded by
the immensity of scientific progress over the years since it
was first published in 1931. But I stopped cold when I came
to an illustration of the comparative sizes of the sun and
the planets of the solar system.

Such straightforward diagrams and illustrations, without artistic embellishment, have always been common in
popular books about astronomy, and they invariably evoke
in most of us a distinct movement inward, a sense of quiet
astonishment, when we pay attention to them.

There, on the photographic plate opposite page 13, the

disc of the sun, white against a black background, occupied nearly half of the large page. Beneath the grapefruit-sized sun, the planets of our solar system were arrayed in two rows ranging in size from mere specks on the page to the relatively larger, but still toylike outer planets—including great Jupiter—the size of marbles in a children's game.

This illustration affected me so strongly not only because it called up the feelings of my childhood about such things. It had also happened that an hour or so before that, while rummaging through the old cartons of books and papers, I had chanced to come across a manuscript that I had forgotten about. It was the translation of a seminal study of the Earth by the renowned Russian geochemist Vladimir Vernadsky, published in 1926. Entitled *The Biosphere,* it showed for the first time that the biosphere of the Earth was an integral dynamic system controlled by life itself. As such, it was the first modern scientific study demonstrating that life was not simply a kind of accidental appendage violating the integrity of a mechanical system, but a defining, actively creative and purposive force shaping the entire physical structure of our planetary world. In the 1970s I had been an occasional member of the team that worked on the English translation, and I had kept for myself a carbon copy of the manuscript. An abridgment and, later, a revised, annotated version of the translation were published bearing the name of the leader of the translation team, the physicist Dr. David B. Langmuir.

It so happened that, not more than an hour before discovering *The Stars for Sam*, I had been reading some passages in the Vernadsky text where the author is discussing the three great regions that constitute the solid part of the Earth underneath the biosphere. With an old, familiar feeling of wonder, I had followed him as he cited the distances down: the "crust" extending forty miles beneath the surface. I paused to imagine that underneath me there were forty miles of solid earth. Then beneath that, a second region extending to a depth of some fifteen hundred miles about which relatively little is known, especially, writes the author, since "the pressure due to the weight above it is so enormous that it defies our imagination and upsets our ordinary ideas of solids, liquids and gases." All right, but *fifteen hundred miles*? That took me aback—I could more or less picture that distance on the surface of the Earth. But fifteen hundred miles *down*? And about which we knew so little? I started feeling, sensing in my imagination, the scale of the size of our planet, like an immense being upon which we human beings crawl like small insects. And when Vernadsky then spoke about the core of the Earth, reaching down to the unknown and unknowable center of our planet some 4000 miles beneath the surface, I could honestly say that I actually felt, with my own sensation and instinctive feeling, the huge massive world upon which I lived along with the whole human species. In short, I was stopped inside my mind, as though my own mind now gave evidence of its own mysterious center on the mere surface of which I had been living my little life.

In that moment I also felt that I myself was a world. An unknown world.

It was with that feeling still echoing throughout the cells of my body that I came upon the diagram showing that the Earth itself, in comparison with the sun, was nothing more than a tiny white speck. From out of the center of my childhood the living memory of my sense of wonder flowed into my thoughts and emotions—an experience that always happened sooner or later every time Elias and I met by the stone wall. And indeed I now saw that it was this sense of wonder—a paradoxical blending of the recognition of our personal nothingness and our sense of the infinite greatness of the cosmos—that was the real unspoken aim of our conversations. When we touched that, or rather when that touched us, as it always did sooner or later, both Elias and I would always stop and share the silence for a very long time.

As I kept looking at the diagram, a new question came to me: What does that mean: *a world*? What is a *world*? Wasn't I now in front of an ancient, timeless idea, an idea, a question I thought I more or less understood, but which now was bursting with unknown life? A world? A world is a *unity*!

This word, *unity,* suddenly took off its outer garment and showed itself to be hugely unknown, and at the same time the goal and aim of all our inner life and purposes. Wasn't unity the aim of our personal search for meaning? Isn't the troubled human condition defined by mankind's fragmentation and disunity? And in the world's spiritual traditions, isn't every great symbol, each in its own way, a symbol of unity and the laws of unity? The word "unity" was now for me no longer an empty and somewhat uninteresting abstract noun. It pulsed with life. It pulsed with mystery. The Earth—the Earth upon which we lived was a great world! And we were part of that unknown world! And we ourselves were also a world!

Yes . . . yes. But: I was not yet a unity; on the contrary. And—was the Earth itself the world that it was meant to be if I, we human beings, were ourselves ridden with disunity and fragmentation? I am not yet a world, therefore the Earth cannot yet be the world it was created to be!

And then, what of the solar system itself and all the other "children of the Sun"? [1]

Thoughts like that, inchoate, passionate, teeming with life, poured through my brain. I needed to think now about all that; I needed to write about the Earth in the light of that great essential question of the meaning of oneness in the universe and in ourselves. I felt a great hope that all the aspects of the question of the Earth—the environment, the human crisis of our relationship to nature and everything that was associated with it—would be seen in a new light from the depths of the great idea of unity in its hard, primal, primordial meaning. All the questions, I felt, all the issues were themselves scattered pieces of an unknown unity waiting to come together under some new, reconciling idea.

I closed the book, unable to keep up with my thoughts. Ah, I felt, if only I could speak to Elias about this!

In fact, that very night I would be seeing him again.

Chapter Three

A Mysterious Directive

Elias appeared in my dream that night exactly as he had been the night before—his large face lined with age and gravity, his black, deep-set eyes burning with steady light. In fact, everything was exactly as it had been: the orange autumn sun low and large in the sky, the shouts of children in the distance, and the low stone wall upon which we were sitting. In every respect the dream seemed to pick up exactly where it had left off—with my soundless outcry echoing in my mind, *Elias! What should we do?*

This fact—that the dream was a continuation of the night before—seemed perfectly natural to me.

Elias tilted his head to the right, as he often used to do after he had challenged me with some question or other. But in this case it was I who had put the question to him.

In the dream-silence we both sat there, each waiting for the other to say something. My thoughts of the day about the Earth seemed slowly to enter the dream—off to the side, not inside my head. As though they, my thoughts, did not belong to me.

I started to repeat my question, *What shall we do?* But in the dream, as it sometimes happens in waking life, entirely unexpected words came out of my mouth and, unlike in the previous night's dream, my words made a sound—it's possible that I even said them aloud in my sleep.

"Are you still dead?" I said.

He just sat there, looking at me with that same mixture of sorrow and disappointment, his head tilted to the side.

"Aren't you allowed to speak?" I said.

He pointed to the ground at my right side, where somehow my thoughts about the Earth were waiting. It was a dream perception, a dream certainty. They, my thoughts, were some kind of beings—I did not imagine any shape or form to them; I did not in the dream question that such a thing could be—one's own thoughts not inside the mind, but outside, perhaps like—who knows what?

"*Put them into your body*," he said. His voice was not the high-pitched voice I remembered. It was an older voice, deeper.

And then he stood up. The sun was beginning to set, getting bigger as it did so, and turning an ever-deepening orange-red. The air was getting colder. And, as sometimes happens in a cloudless sky, it was suddenly dark night. The sun had disappeared beneath the horizon.

He started to walk away. I immediately stood up and followed him, forgetting all about my "thoughts." I stayed beside him, feeling warmth coming from him as the night air became colder and darker. We walked down Franklin Street where the younger children had been playing until, at nightfall, they were called home by their mothers. Although in the dream I was not a younger child, I heard my mother's voice calling me in the distance. It is rare to hear one's own name spoken aloud in a dream, and when it does happen it usually signals awakening. But walking next to Elias, I "chose" not to wake up.

We walked through neighborhoods I had known and lived in as a child even before I had known Elias. We walked a long, long time and finally came to a broad avenue, and as we turned into this wide, empty street, there at the far end of it the sun was now rising, huge and warm and brilliantly whitish yellow. My whole body felt warm and grateful. The voice that had been calling my name sounded again, but it was not from my mother; it was from somewhere else, from someone else.

At that point, Elias took leave.

His face was still full of grief.

I tried to wake up, but I couldn't. Feeling alone, I walked

by myself back through all my childhood neighborhoods. In the dream it took me a long time, and when I returned to the low stone wall the sun was already setting; and again night fell quickly and suddenly. My "thoughts" were still there by the wall.

In my dream I went into my house, the house of my childhood. I went up to my room, undressed and went to bed.

Chapter Four

The Earth Is a Living Being

On awakening, my mind—and I could say my "soul"—was simultaneously inhabited with the blended images, feelings and thoughts from both my daytime and my nighttime: the immensity of the planet Earth and the nearly microscopic white speck that represented the Earth under the great disc of the sun. The huge sun in the dream warming and illuminating me and finally disappearing abruptly, leaving me alone in cold darkness—just as the presence of my dear Elias warmed me and then abandoned me, leaving me to return alone to the low stone wall with only cryptic dream-words to remember him by.

I have to say that for several hours that day it was almost as though I didn't know if I was awake or still asleep and dreaming in bed. My impulse to think and write about the

Earth was chaotically mixed with uncontrollable feelings that must have arisen out of my dream of Elias and the impression of his inexplicable grief. I kept saying to myself that I must hold tightly to the feeling of *love for the Earth*. That was the phrase that kept coming back to me. Never before in my life had I ever thought those words.

Part of me—my more rational part perhaps—started warning me against sentimentality. But when I began to leaf through my books about the Earth and the solar system, some of them purely scientific and technical, the feeling of love for the Earth and—this was totally unexpected— *love for the Sun* kept welling up in me.

My "rational" mind was tugging at me very strongly. I (or it) said to me something like "How interesting! The voice you heard of your mother calling you has been symbolically transformed and symbolized by the Earth, 'Mother Earth.' And the second voice you heard when you saw the sun rising means that for you the sun symbolizes your father, 'Father Sun.' Don't you remember how touched you once were when you encountered in your studies those ritual dances where the voices would chant the 'hymn to the Father Sun'? Don't you remember?"

I knew my "rational mind" was wrong. My feeling for the Earth, and now for the Sun, was not psychological. It was metaphysical, "energetical." Such feelings are quite prior to, earlier than, feelings for one's mother or father.

They are written into the being of man. One could say they exist in us even before we are born. My rational mind, the mind of my externally conditioned personality, never heard of such a thing. If we are fortunate, our actual mother and father act upon us in ways that reflect the nature and the meaning of the Earth and the Sun. Or, if not our actual mother and father, some other blood relative. These connections to the universe—we could speak of it, very cautiously, as God—are in our essence, our blood, not merely in the conditioned personality that is forged from external cultural influences or parental actions.

As the day wore on and the effects of the dream seemed to retreat behind the screen of everyday concerns, difficulties and obligations, I began to understand why the book written by the Russian geochemist Vernadsky had had such a powerful impact upon me. It was not only how he put together the scientific facts and theories about the Earth and the biosphere. It was also, and perhaps even more fundamentally, how he spoke about the Sun.

Let me try to explain this. As most of us know, life on Earth depends on the energy of the sun. It is common to hear it said simply that the heat of the sun's rays, and somehow also, the light of the sun, engender and maintain all of life, or nearly all. Knowing this, and reading it a thousand times in both popular and technical books, I always semiconsciously wondered why it left me so unsatisfied—as though a huge chasm of ignorance was being concealed. How could mere heat or light cause life to appear out of dead matter? More and more sophisticated explanations involving the effect of solar heat and light on the formation and interaction of complex molecules, proteins and amino acids only left me even more unsatisfied.

But Vernadsky's writings, while remaining purely scientific and unsentimental, and while faithfully hewing closely to fact and verifiable observation, communicated something else. At the very beginning of the book, the Russian geochemist writes:

> The face of the Earth viewed from celestial space presents a unique appearance, specific and different from all other heavenly bodies. The surface that separates the planet from the cosmic medium is the *biosphere,* visible principally because of light from the sun, although it also receives from every part of celestial space an infinite number of other radiations, only a small fraction of which are visible to us. We have hardly begun to realize their variety, to understand how defective and incomplete are our conceptions of the world of rays which envelop us, to realize their fundamental importance in surrounding processes, an importance

which is scarcely perceptible to our minds so accustomed to other pictures of the universe.

Not only the biosphere, but all possible space that can be embraced by thought is penetrated by rays from this immaterial domain. These rays are being incessantly propagated around us, within us, everywhere; clashing, following one another, meeting one another.

The perpetual alternation of these space-filling rays already distinguishes these cosmic regions, destitute of matter, from the geometric idea of space as mere emptiness.[2]

Reading these first sentences of the book, I once again recalled the feeling they evoked in me when years before I was sitting in with the team of people working on the translation from the Russian and the French. What were these "infinite number of other radiations" pouring onto the Earth from "every part of celestial space"? Was all of that part of what is more profoundly meant by "the Sun"? Why did these words of Vernadsky now as before send a chill down my spine?

Was life on Earth to be seen as a response from the Earth to its sun-centered universal world? Life a *response*? An *expression*? And, in any case, why did nearly every sentence of Vernadsky's book evoke such thoughts and feelings in me? I had read many texts dealing with astronomy and nature. What was the sensibility of this Russian scientist that enabled him to offer straightforward information in a way that opened the heart even as it informed the mind? It was one thing to be touched like this when directly observing terrestrial nature, the life of plants and animals; and it was one thing to be struck with awe and wonder at the scale of the universe and the starry worlds. But this text was also touching something entirely different in me—and not only in me, but also in each one of the men and women working on the translation.

The thought was, and nowadays has surely become, inescapable: The Earth is a living being. Every living being lives and breathes in an environment; every living being lives and breathes and serves in an environment of all-encompassing life. Every living being has a function in the whole tapestry of organic life.

The Earth is a living being. *Think of it!* I said to myself. Dream of it! Every living being serves . . . from the merest living cell to the great whales and the whole class of insects and . . . man. But also Earth, *Earth itself.* I could not and cannot help but feel the question entering again and again within my being: What is the function, the "good" (as Plato would say), *the purpose of the Earth itself*—and its "word," its *expression,* to which we give the name, *life*?

Chapter Five

Necessary Questions

We know that everything in nature has its unique function, its unique purpose in the biosphere, in the life of the Earth, just as every organ and tissue and class of cells has each its own function, its unique necessary purpose in the organism. But what of the Earth itself? It too is a living being and exists within its own living world, the world of the sun and the planets—and even the stars.

Then what is the purpose of the Earth itself? Where are the people who are asking that question?

For we can be sure: If there is an answer to that question, even the merest beginning of an answer that we can know, then it could transform everything we think and believe about our world and our human life on the Earth, and our death and our own living purpose. All our sense of urgency about the natural world, what we somewhat self-centeredly call the "environment," could change—perhaps like a great song sung in a new key or with subtler tones and notes, or in angelic voices above and below our meager sense of hearing.

I carried that question into my dreams that night.

I am once again ambling, but inwardly hurrying, toward the low stone wall, keeping my eyes open for Elias.

And, sure enough, there he comes, still the man that he had become the first night. Once again, everything in the dream is exactly the same as I left it the night before.

Now, in the dream, I think to myself: This is surely remarkable, the dream again picking up exactly as it left off the night before. I think to myself: This sort of thing never happens in dreams, does it? What does that mean?

Elias sits down on the wall, motioning me to sit close to him.

I quietly sit down and wait. The dream is very clear: I am waiting for . . . myself. I am waiting for myself to express my question about the purpose of the Earth. This waiting is for me a new strangeness, this waiting for my mind to come down to my lips. It feels very important, this waiting. There is no sense of awkwardness about it.

In my dream, I earnestly wish for my expression, my words, to be like the meaning of life on the Earth itself, an arising from silent depths and heights, and not merely words spawned by an agitation in the brain.

I never knew that such subtle impressions could be given in dreams.

Elias is not looking at me; he is looking down at the earth. He is also silent, powerfully silent as usual. But this time it is very clear that his silence is feeding me. I can feel it in my body.

Just then it seems that the dream is abruptly going to end. But I don't want it to end. In order to prevent the dream from ending, in order to stay asleep, I start to say, "What is the purpose of the Earth?" But once again other words than I intended come out of my mouth: "Elias, why did you have to die?"

Still looking down at the earth, he whispers, almost inaudibly: "I am not dead."

With that, I instantly wake up.

But, lying in my bed, I keep my eyes shut, trying to return to the dream. At the same time, I begin to wonder: Why does it happen, I dimly ask myself, that in the dream what I actually say is so different from what I intend to say, so different from what I wanted to ask Elias? But I let that question go. It will return again and again, and with ever greater force.

Other thoughts are swirling in my brain. Everything that lives must die. If the Earth is a living being, it means that the Earth can die. Lying there awake in the darkness of night, I tremble at this thought. I *feel* this thought, this idea that I have heard more than once without understanding it at all. It is an idea implicit in the writings of the great spiritual teacher G. I. Gurdjieff about the purpose of life on Earth. An idea made explicit a hundred times over by his pupil Jeanne de Salzmann.

A hundred times over, she would say that if human beings do not work to become conscious, "*the Earth will fall down.*"

Years had to pass before I slowly began to understand what that meant. At first I thought it had something to do with the need for conscious men and women who were capable of truly intelligent action and who, being conscious in the deepest sense of the word, were capable of carrying out a noble intention amid the chaos and madness in the everyday life of nations and all groupings of what Gurdjieff called "sleeping" human beings. This seemed to me the only rational explanation of her words. Did not every good intention throughout history sooner or later breed faction and conflict? Did not every idealistic social or political movement sooner or later turn into its opposite, spawning conflicting and often violent factions, turning into the very thing it had originally sought to overcome? Only look at what in the sweep of history had become of Christianity, the religion of love, with its inquisitions, crusades and gross political alliances. Look at what was happening to our own social movements, including environmentalism— and even further down to all our little groupings, communal experiments and altruistic organizations! Surely, to care for the Earth, for nature, required men and women deeply free of egoism, especially of the egoism that inevitably covers itself with the masks and façades of "altruism." And even when, say, an honorable movement of social justice eventually won its external goal, what almost always was the ultimate result? Was it anything more than shifting the powers of violence and injustice behind the screen of a new external order where the selfsame destructive forces of malice, fear and resentment soon manifested in different forms?

Obviously, the Earth needed men and women genuinely and permanently free from the forces of egoistic craving and fear!

Was that what she meant when she said that without inner transformation *the Earth will fall down*?

No, that could not be what was meant, not only that. In the first place, there was nothing new in the idea that the world was what it was because man was what he was— inwardly. There was nothing new or extraordinary about the idea that unless people changed, the world would go on as it always has. Of course, what such change meant, the kind and degree of change that was needed—that certainly could be interpreted as extraordinary. But she was not simply saying that the travails of mankind are rooted in human nature—and will not change until human nature changes. She was speaking—and the teaching itself was speaking—not of this or that particular civilization, maybe not even of human life itself.

Not exactly. She seemed to be speaking of the death of a world, a planet, the Earth itself.

Did that mean that life itself would perish without the conscious evolution of human life? Certainly, life had existed for millions of years before the advent of man; but now, somehow, for some reason, it could no longer exist without something that only man could bring. Without it, the Earth could be destroyed. What could that mean?

Earth as a living being could . . . disappear? Could die. As a life dies. And disintegrates. Perishes?

Holding these thoughts while still lying in bed, I closed my eyes and drifted back to sleep.

Elias was there, looking at me with burning eyes. Speaking in a whisper, he said to me:

"Why have you taken so long to come to me?"

I could not answer, so astonished was I by this question. I immediately opened my eyes and turned my head away from the morning sun blazing through my window.

Chapter Six

The Two Faces
of Wonder

What did he mean? Wasn't it Elias who had come to *me*, not I who had come to *him*?

Was I losing my balance? These were only dreams, weren't they? Remarkable dreams, no doubt, but still . . . dreams, not reality. Yet here I was: thinking of Elias-of-my-dreams as real, a real person—not a projection of my own subconscious.

And why, in the dreams, did I never speak out my questions about the Earth to him? Even though each morning I would wake up feeling an increasing sense of urgency to understand what I was calling "the meaning of the Earth." I didn't even consider that phrase as my own invention; it just arose out of my dreams and suddenly appeared in my thoughts. And it seemed so right, even though in a way—at least to my "rational mind"—it made no sense. It made no sense. And yet—the question, the phrase, had for me a strong haunting quality to it. It was as though—yes—there was something about it that seemed strangely familiar to me, as though I had been facing it for a long time, or that I had faced it a long time ago in my life. It had a deeply familiar "taste"—even though on the surface my whole interest in the question was so new and recent!

YES—WHAT DID THIS whole issue remind me of? I stand in front of the Earth and in front of nature, my heart and mind filled with love and wonder, driven into my own being, into my source, my "I am," *remembering*—in the deep Platonic sense of the word—remembering what I am—and seeking to remember the ancient God of I AM within me, even as I look with my "eyes of flesh" at this or that animal, this or that plant, that insect's wing or my own blood cells in the microscopic slide that I myself had prepared in the tenth-grade biology lab—*remembering*—but now in the ordinary sense of the word—the names of the cells—erythrocyte, basophil, eosinophil and more—calling to mind everything that I can recall of their known functions and properties. Or I am gathering together in thought the classification of the flowering plants I am study-ing and the names and functions of their parts, stamen,

pistil, stigma, calyx. . . . Or as a boy of fifteen in the tiny
basement storage room rigged up as a "science closet"
studying the Mendelian genetic ratios of the countless fruit
flies (*Drosophila melanogaster*) that I am breeding—many
of which to my mother's dismay find their way into our
kitchen upstairs.

And more and more, lab after lab, clinic after clinic:
human, animal, worm, insect, fungus, rose, cineraria—
always and ever this double perception of my inner being
and sacred wonder together with the greatness of science
and mathematics and rigorous standards of explanation and verification—the honor code of the honest, good-
minded scientist to accept only what can be seen or touched,
the demand to fight off sentimental theories, ballooning
metaphysical speculations, preposterous pretensions to understand nature without rigorous empirical observation.
These two orders of perception: on the one hand, the silent
wonder of life conjoined with the sensation—like a great
remembered chord—of my own conscious existence; on
the other hand, and at the same time, the expansive, passionate outrush of scientific perception, strictly sense-based
intelligence and joy and care, and the mental task of mas-
tering the mathematics of what I am observing.

And, yes, it was the same thing with nature as such—
which meant to me reality as such, for nature was for me
reality. And therefore it was the same thing with the

Earth—the Earth was reality, was it not? Didn't it all come back to the Earth—wasn't that why in all my childhood talks with Elias at the low stone wall, everything we talked about all came back to the Earth, to nature, to reality—all our talks about the sun and the planets and galaxies and God, and the God before God, and time before time, infinite space, endless time—all of it coming back to scientific facts, facts, truths living in front of us, under us, truth to touch and see and verify, breathe and smell and hear in the wind and rushing water. It all came back to the Earth—the love of nature under the light of what I now see were spiritual, metaphysical ideas about life and death, death as deeply interesting as life—facts, science, geometry, biology, the spinning Earth. The two faces of wonder—one turned to the sky (and God) and the other turned to the Earth (and this reality here and now).

Yes, it was all of one piece, one unity, through my childhood years: two orders of perception, one of which was the felt awareness of what the world speaks of as knowledge about the Earth, and the other what I was experiencing in front of the unanswerable question of what I am and why I myself am here on Earth at all. I see now that thinking and studying about the Earth almost always created in me that mysterious sense of double perception, two kinds of seeing and knowing existing simultaneously and mysteriously in my being.

But that still did not explain why this taste of my thought about the Earth, this twofold taste of both my inner self and my outer knowledge, was so familiar, as though I had begun wrestling with it in my adult years even long after leaving behind my passionate interest in science and biology. Long after I had begun turning my life and my mind toward philosophy and the study of religion.

And suddenly, in one stroke, the answer appears with total clarity. Suddenly—was it only yesterday?—I understand my own words, *the meaning of the Earth.* I understand why the challenge I face in front of both the question and the crisis of the Earth is as familiar and known to me as would be my coming home to a house I was already living in!

How could I have taken so long to see this!

Chapter Seven

The Earth Is
a Sacred Book

Morning. Morning thoughts out from behind the shadows of night.

How could I have taken so long to see this?

The Earth is a sacred book. An ancient idea—found almost everywhere in the ancient worlds, from Pharaonic Egypt to the alchemists and esoteric visionaries of Judaism, Christianity and Islam; to the Taoism of China and the hidden doctrines and practices in the mountains of Tibet and in the surpassingly great cultures of India; to the powerful spiritual teachings of tribal cultures throughout the Americas, Africa, Asia: Nature in all its diversity as the signature of God and, indeed, the "language" of God. A language that has both an inner and an outer meaning, *like scripture itself.* Like scripture itself, Nature can be "read" in its outer, literal meaning and at the same time intuited in the many levels of its symbolic, transcendent meaning. Like scripture itself, like the language of God itself, Nature, the Earth calls man to the heights and depths of uniquely human double perception, inner and outer simultaneously, drawing him outward to expression and engagement in the world at the same time that it calls him upward, inward, toward the silent inner Self or God within.

For a half century of my life, I have been studying and teaching about sacred texts—Bible, Sutra, Upanishads, legend, symbol—at their origin encoded writings demanding to be understood or "heard" with both the outer and the inner sense of hearing; seen with both the eyes of flesh and the eyes of fire. To take such texts in their purely literal meaning can be a transforming experience, true, but only within the inner fire of transcendent faith. Apart from that, such sacred writings call us to the search for an inner state of listening (Christ's "ears to hear")—listening, attention that is not only of the mind, but also of the heart. But even then not only of the mind and the heart, but also— and of paramount importance, an importance that has been tragically forgotten—*a new attention of and from within the physical body.*

Seen in this light, we can say that *science offers us a literal reading of the language of God.* It shows us outer nature as nature appears to the outer man; the outer Earth as the Earth appears to the outward-directed mind—the mind that is dependent on the outward-directed five senses, together with the automatisms of mental logic (mathematics) along with the ability to combine sense-based impressions in ever new and original ways.

And it is in the light of this uniquely human capacity of double perception that we can glimpse the possibility of both a deeper appreciation and a sharper criticism of the materialism of modern science—a sharp criticism and a deep appreciation of how modern science approaches reality, the universe, our body and our Earth.

To begin with, we need to make a distinction between science and what is called "scientism." Science itself is, at its own level, a truly honorable method of investigating nature. It is fundamentally *empirical*, that is, based on actual observation and personal experience, observations and experience that can be tested and repeated by others under strictly defined external conditions. It brings us remarkable and essential knowledge, but it is knowledge gathered and synthesized by only one of the cognitive powers of the human psyche. Such knowledge may be great and powerful in its rightful domain. But it is not the same thing as *understanding* in the full sense of the word. And the crisis of our present relationship to the Earth is evidence of the danger of knowledge without understanding.

What is called "scientism" is the unwarranted extrapolation of the scientific method into realms it cannot, by its very nature, enter. It appears when scientific knowledge presumes to have the sole authority to dispose of all fundamental questions. But there are questions that require another quality of consciousness. Such fundamental questions are sometimes called "unanswerable": questions of meaning and purpose, the existence of God, good and evil—all of the great questions of the heart that are the main concerns of real philosophy and authentic religion. It may be true that they are unanswerable, but only by one part of the mind alone.

Understanding is a capacity of the whole of the human psyche. There are fundamental problems and questions of human life that cannot be resolved by organizing outward perception alone, but which simultaneously and inescapably require the active energy of inner perception. The question of our relationship to the Earth is one of these fundamental questions.

WE ARE GOING to see that the danger of scientism is the same as that of the dogmatically literal-minded reading of scripture. Just as the error of dogmatically taking sacred texts too literally is that the individual is not aware that he or she is hearing them with only a part of the whole human psyche, so also science becomes scientism not because it relies so much on the senses and mental logic, but because it does not go toward the world with the fullness of sensing—with the energy of the outward-directed mind informed by the energy of the inward-directed mind, with its unique power of non-egoistic intuition and feeling. The revolution in our understanding of the Earth requires that we seek to inhabit the physical with more, not less, of our psyche.

If the Earth is a living being, as it surely is, then, like everything that lives, it is either growing or dying. But perhaps, in ways that we do not understand, in order to grow, the Earth needs our uniquely human conscious energy.

Many ancient writings speak of the Earth as an angel. But perhaps the Earth is the embryo of an angel, an angel on the way to being born.

Chapter Eight

The True Human Body

What is the Earth? Is it a thing? An object?

To call it a thing or an object makes the Earth too small, smaller than man, smaller, even, than myself, here, now. A "thing" has no essential life; and as for an "object," no—an object is something apart from me, other than me, also without essential life, something I can use to serve my purposes, whatever they may be, or else something I can discard physically or in thought—or merely something I happen to be directing my attention to, without implying anything at all about its nature or reality, or what kind of attention it requires and deserves from me.

The Earth is much greater than that—not only in size, but in . . . in what? Greater in what sense? And here the question insists itself: What quality of attention do I need

THE TRUE HUMAN BODY 39

to bring to this Earth?—truly as though it were a sacred book. The answer to that question will show us what we now desperately need to know about what the Earth is.

This question of what quality or level of attention I bring to whatever happens to be in my field of experience—this defining measure of reality has not been taught in our sciences or in our philosophies or religions.

But what is this that I have stumbled upon? In fact I have never heard levels of reality defined or measured in this way—as corresponding to the quality of attention required of me.

But isn't this notion just what I have come to under-stand in my relationship to my own body? Doesn't my body, until then an unconscious "something," come alive when touched and penetrated by a deeper quality of attention? And doesn't the quality of our everyday life mirror this quality of relationship between our mind and our body?

And isn't our body our own private, personal "Earth"?

It is so, isn't it? If the body can come alive, transform its state, serve my deeper aims, heal itself when flooded with conscious attention; if the body can do, act, love with entirely new force and joy when it is filled with conscious attention, then we may say that the Earth itself will be a new Earth when human beings see her, hear her, taste her with the conscious attention that only human beings can bring to her. Such attention is not the pale, powerless, thin witnessing that the word "attention" often denotes. Conscious attention is a force that, if only for a moment, lifts the being of whatever or whomever it touches. The great secret of what the Earth needs from us is here.

Humanity's relationship to the Earth mirrors our own essential relationship to our own physical body.

Who is it that lives on and in this personal Earth, this human body I call mine? How do I regard this, my own Earth? What do I do with it, what do I demand of it as I go about my life? What quality of attention do I give to it? And in those moments when life becomes infinitely more real, when I become infinitely more present, when *I* become real, when time transforms, is it true that there comes into being an entirely new relationship to the body? Perhaps it is truer to say: an *entirely new body* emerges for a moment from behind the shadows of my tensions and anxieties; from behind my obsessions and fantasies; from behind the big little storms of hurt feelings and wounded vanity—all of which is to say: from behind my egoism, that egoism, that *ego,* which inhabits and exercises unwarranted dominion over this personal Earth I call the body—not unlike the planet-wide ego of the Earth which is unawakened man.

But in those rare moments—be it of sudden danger, or grief, or inexpressible joy, or sometimes for no reason at all—in those moments the ego evaporates under the sun of a new attention, and the body receives a new influence that

THE TRUE HUMAN BODY

awakens a new life in every cell, tissue and muscle. The body finds its mind and its heart. At last! No longer is it being fed the straw of craven pleasure, no longer is it being whipped by tensions. No longer is this Earth that is my body being forced to flee in terror from phantom enemies of the ego's imagining. No longer are the body's immense energies being mined and plundered by the illusions of that blind, false master, the ego. In that precious moment, evidence of a true authority has appeared, evidence that the true human body can exist. Evidence of what we are meant to be.

Such fragile evidence! Evidence, meaning, unknown and unrecognized by the world around us. No sooner does it appear than, in its most familiar moments, it disappears like a shy mythical being. In fact, we will eventually discover that it can exist in us only when it is deeply needed and can be seen only as we allow ourselves to be seen by it.

In fact, *it,* this true authority, never disappears; it is we who disappear as the ego flies out from the shadows to re-usurp its unrightful place. Very soon, the body recognizes that the blind master has returned, and this poor exploited body forgets what it has just known of joyful obedience. And it returns to its hidden, sullen mastery, pulling the self-deluded ego through the ego's dangerous dreams of power, fear and toxic pleasure, this poor body, this poor personal Earth in which the ego despoils the very thing that is pulling the strings of its own self-destructive existence. For ultimately the body rules the ego even as the ego despoils the body. Such is the sinister symbiosis of our common life.

This poor ego has no idea that everything it yearns for—love, respect, safety, happiness—can be had only through the influence of the new attention, which is now lost to sight and which, perhaps for only a moment, for only a fleeting moment, brought with it a new sun and a new Earth in one's own individual life.

This experience has many levels. There is an inconceivable range of heights and depths waiting for us in our life on this personal Earth. Which is also to say that there is a place on planet Earth waiting for us—a place called Man. The Earth, Great Nature itself, is waiting for us to become what such experiences, however fleetingly, indicate as our possibility.

Nearly every one of us can identify at least one such vibrantly remembered moment that points us to the human future.

Here is one of mine.

Chapter Nine

A Metaphysical Event

It is late in the afternoon, October 17, 1989. I am sitting at my desk preparing my class for the next day, Wednesday. I have only a vague memory what class it was that I was preparing—it may have been a seminar I was teaching, a comparative study of the Tibetan Buddhist text *The Life of Milarepa* and the sermons of the Christian mystic Meister Eckhart.

Five o'clock was approaching and I had promised myself that I would take a break to watch the World Series. I do remember that without the slightest sense of contradiction or remorse, I allowed deep spiritual ideas and their attendant feelings to be wiped from my mind by the television which I clicked on as I sank into the armchair next to my desk.

The commercials came to an end and the pre-game formalities got under way as both teams took the field. I sank even farther back in the armchair in a blurred haze of childlike anticipation. My body was nowhere to be found. Nor was my mind. The Oakland A's had beaten the San Francisco Giants in the first two games, and so I eagerly awaited the Giants' comeback now that they were at their home field, Candlestick Park. All was well. All manner of things were well.

In the middle of the introductions, as the players one by one were running onto the field, I started sliding off the chair. No problem. Then I heard a deep grinding sound coming from everywhere—what the hell!—as I continued to slide, and as I did what I could to keep from falling to the floor. The television screen went blank. I heard some objects falling somewhere and I tried and failed to stand up and then I struggled with all my might to stand up and when I did the floor slanted and I slanted the other way while everything shook and rolled and the rumbling, grinding sound continued for what seemed a long, long time. Weaving violently back and forth, I staggered toward the door to my office and as I made it to the door, thoughts of what to do in an earthquake were immediately eclipsed by concerns for my wife, who was also somewhere in the house. The image of the roof caving in flashed through my mind along with the possibility of a breaking gas pipe and my wife's and my own possible injury and even death.

I felt no fear whatever. That is to say, I was aware of the thoughts and images of destruction wriggling in my head like a tangle of worms. Yet my body suddenly became deeply relaxed and full of another kind of force under the influence of which I moved with great dexterity and speed to find my wife. All the while I sensed and felt an immense reality moving beneath my feet. Quietly, gently, I said to myself: "This is the Earth, this is the planet moving—one little twitch of the Earth and I am like a bug on the back of an elephant. This is a *planet*!" I could almost say I sensed and felt its mass, its weight, its being—that is, the scale of its being, that it occupied an entirely different cosmos than I did, than we did, than did all of mankind. I experienced throughout my body a profound sense of wonder that such a movement as this could in one moment take away every-thing in my life, everything in the life around me. Yet I felt no fear. On the contrary, even with the squirming images of destruction still in my head, I felt a powerful impulse of quiet freedom passing through my solar plexus and my arms and legs and torso like a cooling zephyr. It was as though I were being liberated to do whatever it was that I was meant to do on this Earth, in this life. To say I experi-enced and verified the ancient idea of the impermanence of all things would be to put an all-too-familiar label on an inconceivable feeling of a scale incommensurate with all the emotions that color our everyday life.

This was the new attention—or a fundamental step toward it. And this was the new world I was in. And this was the new Earth—both personal and planetary. No, the Earth is not a thing, not an object.

The Earth is a being. Simply that, nothing less, nothing more—and there is nothing more than *to be*. There is nothing more than *being*. Formless, all-powerful being in all its emptiness and fullness. Empty, it is full; full, it is empty, not yet differentiated, not yet poured into the world of things with names. As it is said in the Upanishads, "words turn back."[3]

But it was the aftermath of the earthquake that completed the evidence we are speaking of. After the quake and some of the aftershocks subsided, and after Gail and I walked around the house to look for damage; and after we learned a little about some of the effects throughout the city, I opened the front door and stepped outside. Silence. It was the silence of a cathedral. Cars with doors flung open sat in the street—still as sculptures. The air pregnant and tender. Fallen trees and branches frozen in their places like beings who had just seen God.

Huge October sun touching the horizon, sending rays of

dark gold light halfway up the sky through the hanging dust.

But it was the people, then and in the days that followed.

Then and in the days that followed, as I went about my business, I could hardly believe I was in the same world I had lived in before. It was not just that during those days my state of being continued to reflect the action of the earthquake upon me. I mean to say that although the new attention I had experienced during the temblor had not lasted more than a few seconds, the ego did not immediately come back as it almost always does in one form or another. That was striking, but not uncommon: Something similar happens to many of us at the loss of a loved one— days, weeks and even months can pass before the state of God-given fully human grief is eclipsed by more familiar emotions of fear, self-pity, guilt, anger or avarice. But in this case what was now truly remarkable was that during these few days the whole city of San Francisco seemed to remain in a state of profoundly diminished egoism.

Sometimes I noticed this first in myself and sometimes I noticed it first in others. For one thing, I saw that I was never in a hurry—and soon enough I observed the same thing in other people. It was not that I walked or moved or spoke more slowly. It was only that inwardly I was never nervously ahead of what was happening in the moment.

Even if I had to move fast, I was never *in a hurry*, inside myself. And I detected this also in the people around me, even in crowded streets.

And speaking to people, especially in extended conversations, I soon realized that they—and I myself—hardly ever interrupted. People just listened. I felt it, and they must have felt it too. There was no tense waiting for an opening in order to have one's say or refute the other or outshine him, or get something off one's chest.

In addition, people waited in long lines without nervousness.

Doors were opened for others and not only men opening doors for women.

People passed each other on the street feeling free to smile or say hello or say nothing at all.

Everywhere, with very few exceptions, there was unforced courtesy, civility.

Of course, we should be careful not to make more of all this than it deserves, but it is even more important that we not make less of it than it deserves. In these seemingly mundane details of a day or two following a major earthquake, thousands of men and women were sensing, knowing, *in the body*, things that people—and relatively few of us at that—sometimes recognize only mentally or emotionally: namely, that nothing in our lives rests on solid ground. We live and breathe and conduct our lives on this Earth and this Earth can move and when it moves it can take everything and everyone with it. This Earth is a being, a being of unimaginable immensity and power. It cares nothing for our buildings, our houses, our cities, our technologies, our proud nations and monuments—our little toys, our pieces of paper or gold. And what is more: This twofold perception of the outer world and the inner state of the self, sensed in the mysterious whole of our being, sensed in the body and the mind and the heart working together, this perception, this knowing, extends also to our very private "possessions": our thoughts, which we value so highly and which we trust to guide and plan our lives and prepare our souls for the future; our loves and hates; our sense of place in time and history, in the annals of our vaunted culture and civilization—a civilization which, in fifteen seconds more or less, with one twitch of the crust of the Earth, can be transformed into broken pillars of stone and twisted steel.

Inwardly and outwardly the city was shaken to its roots. This was not only a geological event; it was a metaphysical event, an event that begs for metaphysical understanding, just as what took place within each individual demands metaphysical understanding. Both the city and its people experienced the shock of destruction—that in fact for a moment liberated the people of the city from the thrall of illusion, exposing us to and also freeing us from our emotional and physical attachments. We were transformed.

Is all this a glimpse of what we need to require of our lives?—for the mind to come down into the body, the mind with all its hopes and values and ideals to come down into the body which is built to obey genuine conscience— built to accept and willingly obey only what corresponds to great life and its purposes?

Earth: Is this what you need from your children of the sun?

As I think these thoughts rooted in the past, I begin to remember Elias.

Chapter Ten

A Real Question
Is a Seed

But that night Elias did not appear. I went to bed expecting him, but no sooner did my head touch the pillow than my eyes opened to the gray light of morning.

I began the activity of the day quietly with no sense of disappointment. The rare night of dreamless sleep brought with it a relaxed sense of confidence and trust. I had found my question, my nest of questions, about the Earth. And they had brought with them questions about myself, my own life. I recognized that we cannot speak about the Earth without at the same time speaking about ourselves. We cannot understand what the Earth is and is meant to be without questioning what we ourselves are and are meant to be. If our planet is in crisis, as it surely is, it is because we ourselves are in crisis, because we ourselves have lost our way in this world. And if we are to find a real and not self-deceptive understanding of the crisis of the Earth, we are going to have to find a real understanding of the crisis of our human life, both our inner life of the mind and the life of action and relationship.

It is customary to think that a sense of security and confidence comes from finding an answer, rather than a question. But the sense of security initially brought by "answers" almost always proves to be illusory. Taken in our usual state, answers soon close the mind and in so doing strengthen egoism, breeding conflict and yet more difficulties in our individual and collective lives. Human history, with its endless barbarism, could even be seen as the history of answers and their bloody progeny. And, in a way, it is the same also in one's own personal life. Collectively and individually, we do not suffer (or commit) evil because of our questions, but because of our answers.

A question, a real question, one's own question, often torn from subterranean depths within ourselves, humanizes us, opens the mind and heart to receive and not to inflict, concentrates the attention and gives our lives an aim. Just as in the objective world of nature, real hunger implies the existence somewhere of food, and just as a seed naturally falls or is carried to where there is nourishment, so one's own real question is meant to grow into a living truth. A real question is a seed—a seed that requires tending and nourishment.

How to tend this question about the meaning of the Earth? How to offer it the nourishment of new experiences or insights guided at first by thoughts, memories, information, ideas from one's own mind and from the work of others?

With this aim, I begin gathering books from everywhere in the house, stacking them at the sides of my desk next to the writings of Vernadsky and the beloved *The Stars for Sam*.

Here are the sobering writings of James Lovelock offering his vision of the living and dying Earth as Gaia,[4] the ancient Greek goddess of Earth and land—along with books by scientists, naturalists, journalists and philosophers influenced by this vision. Here, too, are the eloquently alarming proclamations of Bill McKibben[5] and others who by their own lights tell us, as does Lovelock, that it is already too late to avert planetary catastrophe. Here, also, are more optimistic, and, to my mind, more dubious writers recommending ever more extreme ways to engineer our way through the crisis—or at least buy time until our culture deeply accepts what is really at stake, or until the inevitable appearance of as yet unforeseen breakthrough technologies that will rescue our life on Earth.

And here as well are humanistic and spiritually sensitive writings that survey the crisis with a challenging but realistic element of hope, including the magisterial study by Gregg Easterbrook, *A Moment on the Earth*,[6] and Thomas Berry's *The Great Work*.[7]

And, again, here are books—books flying into my hands from everywhere in my house—books blending pure love of nature with poetic vision or with acute philosophical analysis or scientific expertise: David Abram's *The Spell of the Sensuous*[8] is here, for example, and also the great classic of deep, warm science, Guy Murchie's *The Seven Mysteries of Life*,[9] and many, very many others.

I had no idea it would be like this. But of course it had to be. Every book I owned about nature was finding its way onto the shelves near my desk. And not so near: I find myself moving what seems like hundreds of fat and thin books around my now overcrowded office in order to make room for more and more old paperback and hardcover friends and fond acquaintances, all of them fiercely relevant whether or not they mention even once the word "ecology" or "environment"—or even "crisis," or even "earth."

At the same time, books, some rather heavy, are dropping on my feet as I move things around. Entire shelves are being dislodged, some even falling off their braces and tumbling onto the floor as I try to make room for what I will need for my work. Where will I put all these books? And are there any of my books that *aren't* relevant? I am half laughing, half worrying that I am drowning.

Here, for example, is the magnificent study by Henry Corbin, the great scholar of Islamic mysticism. The title of the book is mesmerizing: *Spiritual Body and Celestial Earth.*[10] The subject is nothing less than the fusion of spirit and matter as experienced in spiritually lucid states of human consciousness, the attainment of which was historically among the aims of Iranian Sufism. In these teachings, the planet Earth is not primarily perceived through the senses, nor understood by logically organizing sensory impressions, as is done by modern science. Another inner, metaphysical perception of the Earth is given that shows its place in a universe both of infinite space and of infinitely higher purposes: a perception of the Earth that is given only in more lucid, deeper states of human consciousness. In this book, Corbin introduces us to the written form by which this vision of the Earth was originally presented: a literary form in which a mythical figure offers what is called a "visionary recital." In these visionary recitals, legendary prophets chart an esoteric geography in which the Earth we see is but a reflection in a mirror. In these recitals our entire Earth is shown to exist on the mere surface of a reality within which are not only unimaginable material forces, but also invisible meanings of the world we tread with our feet and see with our "eyes of flesh."[11]

DAYS AND WEEKS PASS. I am reading, reading. My entire intellectual life is passing before my eyes. More and more, the question of the Earth touches everything—everything I have known or studied or dreamt about in my life. Buddhism? A hundred Buddhist books are calling to me as they migrate from their comfortable shelves upstairs down to the walls and floor of my formerly spacious study: Zen Buddhism with its deconstruction of Western rationalism and its spiritual practice of concentrated, pure awareness. And a hundred Tibetan Buddhist texts are rushing to join them, singing to me in chords that magically unlock the purest states of human consciousness, releasing into the air the greater mind's nuclear mythic symbols—gods and demons—radiating guidance and compassionate ferocity through the universal world and into the tissues of the transforming human body and, through our bodies, into the body of our hungry Earth. The Buddha saying to me, to us, that our Earth, biological nature, mountain, forests and oceans have been created out of—out of . . . what? Out of ignorance! Out of our deluded minds and tormented hearts! What can that mean? What can that possibly mean?

And one by one, two by two, inch by inch, the sacred books of India gather themselves together—ancient companions of my youth, now claiming their rightful place. "All along, we, too, have been speaking to you of the Earth," they say, "but you have not been able to hear us!" My memory now reaches back to India's great idea of the universal Self, the Atman, within man: the Self we really are, hidden behind the self we pretend to be; the Self also called Brahman, the Absolute, *God*—the heart and Mind of reality. Could this be also the reality that waits behind our science's sad quarks and neutrinos whirling in paradoxical patterns, telling us the same thing again and again as we go down ever deeper into ever smaller, ever more invisible elements of matter where the blunt materiality of the world dissolves into a mirror of our mind and consciousness?—mind and consciousness including everything at one and the same time, including all our logic and mathematics, all seen and fecundated by the One Watcher called Purusha, the Self, the Golden Person. This, this Purusha along with its metacosmic mate, Prakriti, a word signifying the transcendent principle of materiality, of which what we helplessly call "matter" is but a secondary derivative. Speaking to our world, India says to the Earth (and to me): "Earth, you are a crossroads. You, Earth, you (addressing me) with your human body, your human Prakriti, are a place of decision, a place where beginnings and endings are

born. What path will you choose to follow?—toward God
or toward extinction? The path of the Sun or the path of
the Moon?[12] Where, Earth, do you, and where, Man, do
you wish to go? It is here, now, on this material plane, that
the choice must be made."

Why had I never heard this before in the teachings of
India? Why did I hear the doctrine of the great Self only as
dreamy metaphysical idealism? Why, for me, had the idea
of the great Self served only as a source of vague conso-
lation, nothing more than an interesting philosophical
theory? Why did I never hear this idea as an immediate personal demand, an arrow aimed at my heart and will, the
heart and will of man, and the heart and will of the Earth
which has brought forth man?

BUT NOW, what are these even more than hundred books?
Must I really find room for them as well? The question
wells up from some forgotten depth. *Judaism!* Judaism,
haven't I already made my peace with you, religion of my
childhood? Have I not felt the immensity of your demand
upon me, recognizing that this demand was there even
before I was born—this mysticism of your moral com-
mandments, your never once asking me to make an independent choice, God having created me already in my

mother's womb under immense obligation. And, yes, you know that I joyfully accepted the freedom you thrust upon me without asking my permission, unlike religions which may seem to treat man as an outsider invited to choose to enter the sphere of the eternal? And now, as I write, are you asking me to understand that when you speak of a holy land, it is not a mere portion of geography that you have offered us, but a land waiting somehow to be *made* holy by us? This holy land—is it perhaps *the Earth itself*?

But what of the dominion over nature and the Earth that you have granted us,* a dominion that has been trumpeted and organized throughout history through the mighty Christianity that emerged from your loins? Were you, Judaism, and your immense child really responsible for our culture's obsession always and everywhere to master and then exploit our Mother Earth? Again and again you have been so accused—because of that which began there in the legendary Garden when the Lord gave us the Earth and its creatures to serve us. There, so we have heard, is where the crime began—all our criminal exploitation of animal life and green plants, the minerals and stones and energies of the Earth, the Earth and its waters and its sacred air and its

* Psalm 8.

subterranean veins of congealed sunlight—gold, copper, iron—all of them.

Yet this accusation so often hurled against you, Judaism and Christianity, is it not in fact one of the toxic lies that pollute the modern mind even as the poisons we invent pollute the food we eat and the air we breathe? For what did the Lord really mean when he spoke of man's "dominion" over nature, over "every living thing"?[13] Your well-intentioned defenders may argue that we were given the Earth to be as stewards, preservers. But they too are victims of the lie. Have we not, all of us, forgotten, that the Lord gave man the function of dominion over of the life of the Earth only insofar as he is the servant of God? We are to care for nature and even to perfect nature only as we become able to receive the divine energy of the Creator—first inwardly and then outwardly. The true emissary of the king, above all, does the will of the king in the land that belongs to the king.

But what does man serve, what do we obey, when we no longer obey the Creator, when we no longer serve or even recognize the higher conscious energies waiting to enter our lives? For nothing in the universe exists alone. Everything obeys something. And if we do not obey God, then what do we obey? Inwardly, the answer is: the infernos of craving, fear, hatred, the icy logic of illusion and self-will. Outwardly, the answer is to be discovered not only in the gaping wounds we have inflicted on nature, but ultimately in the genocides and in the trails of unimaginable anguish carved out in space by our orbiting planet of war.

READING . . . READING. Days pass, weeks, months. The great and near-great books of my life absorb me one by one. They speak to me in a new voice because I now have a new mind that can understand them in a new way. Great and near-great ideas one by one sweep over the tracks they have left as they passed through my mind when I was young, tracks often petrified in the now desiccate ground of the past. Mere tracks of huge living ideas, residing now in my mind only as forms and words. I see that I have loved such ideas as a young man loves a fascinating woman, never seeing her entire humanity. Ideas we fall in love with, but never join with in marriage, never commit the whole of ourselves to the whole of them. Never did I see all the aspects of these great and near-great ideas of my past; always I have lived with only one or two aspects, which is like living with only one or two aspects of someone I thought I loved. But now . . . now . . . now I somehow see them more fully and bow my head before them. No idea exists alone. Every idea is part of a whole world of thought and insight—how is it that I did not understand *that*, as I fell in love with one after another? Such indiscriminate love! Such impatience! Such youth! Never did I even imagine that it was possible and necessary to let real ideas come down inside me—*to enter my body.*

And instantly as I think these words I am haunted by a presence in the air about me.

Chapter Eleven

Mind and Nature

Reading . . . reading. Days pass, weeks, months.
Here they are: Freud—reaching down into my sense of wonder not only at the sky above me, but now toward the mind within me. Not only my own discovery, but the discovery of our entire culture, the discovery, the idea that I live only on the surface of my mind, that there is an unfathomed consciousness within me unknown to my "conscious" self. Here the great idea of India, the idea of the unknown Self within us, again heaves into view, an immense vessel of an idea whose prow bears the name of psychoanalysis and whose true dimensions are beginning to appear as our culture glimpses the vastness of the unknown world within. In this idea of Freud I feel—the modern world around me feels—the Earth and great

nature herself as part of my mind, even the essential part of the mind. I am not only what I call a man—and what that is I do not know—but I am also nature, biological, earthly. I am nature, I have the animal within my mind, animal desire, animal need—it is not only my body that is biological, it is my identity, my sufferings and sense of identity. Yes, here is Freud saying to his pupil, the Swiss psychiatrist Ludwig Binswanger: "Man has always known he possessed spirit; I had to show him there is such a thing as instinct."[14] We are Earth, we are nature.

The passage of time, of course, shriveled this idea into a brand of reductionism. But for decades its greatness opened our eyes, however much it later closed them, to the great question: What is Man? Who am I? Now, once again, like a man returning to a first love, I see the young life behind the pale lineaments of old age: Yes, we are of the Earth. But also, we . . . are . . . of the heavens. In my mind, reading Freud, I feel the weight of the ancient idea of man's two natures. How difficult it is to hold on to that great and ancient idea! How difficult to give each its true weight. How easy to dismiss what everyone calls "dualism"! As though it were an error instead of a great truth. Only this great truth can give real sacred power to the ultimate idea of man's possible unity—true man containing both the gravity of Earth and the energies of Heaven.

And here is the once widely honored, but now everywhere despised seventeenth-century philosopher René Descartes—despised now for conceiving of the mind as utterly separate from matter, and therefore from the body and therefore from nature and the Earth. But I am now reliving the thrill I felt when I first read his exercise in pure thought, thought unmixed with sense perception. Commentators now revile this exercise of his. They hate him, but they cannot understand or perceive what Good, knowingly or not, he was bringing to the emerging modern world.

Descartes writes that he is looking for certainty.[15] Certainty—not blind belief that masquerades as certainty, but which is almost always self-suggestion. He is looking for absolute certainty—about something, anything. He is willing to go anywhere in his mind, think anything, just to have one experience of absolute certainty. And so with this aim, he tries his famous, now infamous, exercise: He withdraws his mind from any activity in which what is known can possibly be doubted. Anything. He recognizes that anything he believes because of sense perception could conceivably be false—for, as he observes, we are often deceived by sense perception—and to show this he traverses absolutely everything we generally take as obviously true. And, ruthlessly setting aside—bracketing, as it were—all possible perceptions and beliefs that we take as self-evident, he ends by seeing that there is one and only one thing that is indubitably certain—the fact, the experience, that he—that is, *I* exist now and here thinking these thoughts, making this experiment. For even if I am deceived even here, even if some evil god is entering my brain and deceiving me, still it is I who am being deceived, I who am thinking these thoughts (whether they are true or not). And with this, he delivers his famous (now also infamous) absolute certainty: *I think therefore I am.* Rooted in this certainty, Descartes ingeniously ends by arguing for the utter separateness between two realities: the reality of mind and the reality of nature. He then argues that the only thing that can harmonize these two separate kinds of reality is a force from above, a third thing: namely, God.

All this has had a huge influence in modern thought, vitalizing the whole scientific revolution with its methods of knowing nature that, along with other great influences, now still define the culture in which we all live and breathe and take our sense of identity.

And now he is despised for creating the rupture between mind and matter—between man and nature.

But that is not at all what he was doing. His great exercise of seeking for certainty actually represents the emergence of a power of the human mind that was being covered over by the decaying Christian world. What he was showing, and what I was experiencing reading him at a time when I was only a precociously philosophical teenager, was the possibility of the human mind to withdraw its attention into itself, to separate the mind from all that pulls it outward, to intensify its power of attention into a pure light. What thrilled me, and what thrilled or astounded so many, was the invitation to develop that which is uniquely the power of a human being. We call that power *concentration*: the power to withdraw the attention of the mind away from all that is offered to it by the senses and the emotions, along with all thoughts and images that are rooted in either sense perception or emotion.

Of course, anyone who tries to think seriously or work seriously at any craft or task or question brings to his work at least some of the power of concentrated attention. But the problem is that we are absolutely swept away by the *results* of this power—the accomplishment that this power of attention enabled us to reach. We do not value enough or understand rightly what this power of concentration tells us about what we are and what we are meant to be.

What Descartes is showing us is something dramatically different from how he has been interpreted: He is showing us that in the capacity of the mind to concentrate its attention toward itself in pure thought—in that capacity there is a central element of Man that is not merely separate from nature, but *beyond nature*! Beyond Earth!

What Descartes is offering is neither more nor less than the idea of the holy spirit expressed not in religious language, but in the language of the independent human mind, the aspect of man that is, in inception, in its embryonic form, beyond the created world of nature, beyond the Earth.

And, what is even more astonishing, he is showing us that the element in Man that is beyond Earth, beyond nature, is meant, ultimately, to manifest outward and downward *into* nature, *into* Earth—in the form of embodied knowledge, understanding. His experiment is a halting first step in the true separation which is a precondition for true unity. As the ancient alchemists knew, one must first separate rightly before rightly joining together.

The vision that would lead to the birth of modern science was the vision of a deep power of the human mind penetrating nature, the Earth and the human body.

But this incipient vision never survived or grew beyond its birth. A strange sort of failed twin embryo was also born at the same time. It had the look of Descartes' great discovery, but none of its essential power or goodness. Like a mythic dark twin, it stole the food meant for the embryonic human soul. We are going to see that the first origins of modern science can be interpreted as the first step in an *aborted* process that originally pointed to the power of human consciousness to truly care for nature and the Earth. We are going to see that this power was almost immediately usurped by (or degraded into) its mere simulacrum and became the power and the ambition to exploit the Earth.

Did Descartes know anything of this interpretation of his experiment? I think not. Would he have even considered it had it been presented to him? Perhaps, but perhaps not. But it does not matter. What matters is our own experience and understanding and what they can show us about an entirely new kind of relationship between consciousness and nature, between consciousness and the Earth, between consciousness and the human body here, now, in our lives.

Chapter Twelve

The Philosophy of the Earth

More books, more philosophers. I am beginning to sense a profoundly new and unexpected relationship to the great thinkers who have accompanied me throughout my life—and with it, a completely new sense of the meaning and the function of philosophy itself. Having had the good fortune, the blind luck, that enabled me vividly to call to mind my first actual, personal inner experience reading Descartes, which has given me an understanding of his significance unlike any interpretation in the scholarly books, I was prepared to apply the same approach to the other major philosophical writings that have influenced Western thought. That is, I prepared myself to try to re-experience what actual "neurological" process took place in my own general psyche when I first studied these thinkers.

To engage in this approach would require that I separate myself from associating about the content of their arguments, just as I had done when I called to mind my first experience reading Descartes. This would require that I set aside, or at least dampen, all concerns and interests relating to the ultimate truth or falsity of the writings of the philosophers. In doing this, I would try to bring back the impression of how my mind and heart and even my bodily sensations operated as I read them. I was quite sure that alongside all the usual kinds of associative, logical, conceptual, emotional reactions to their writings and ideas, there also had proceeded in me a quiet, nearly invisible movement of attention and energy that was, so to say, the unique signature of the effect each writer had upon me and which, perhaps, constituted a fundamental element determining their influence in the culture at large. In a word, I would try to observe how each philosopher affected my state of consciousness—which is a quite different factor than belief, explanatory power, social significance, etc.—the usual markers of how ideas and arguments are judged.

But in addition to this radical approach, there was in me the fundamental faith that there could be no great truth, no great ideas, no real philosophy or fundamental scientific or religious thought that was not deeply relevant to the question of man's relationship to the Earth. Would thinking that way be what is now in scholarly circles called by the ugly word "presentism"—that is, the error of applying strictly contemporary perspectives in interpreting past events or writings? Well, yes, of course, what we call the "environment" is primarily a contemporary issue. But the Earth? Nature?—that has always been and always will be at the heart of all serious human thought—even if the word "environment" or even "earth" is never once mentioned.

Recollecting the experience of my own mind in reading Descartes, I glimpsed an essential aspect of the human mind that transcended everything that we ordinarily call "nature," and that justifies Descartes' sundering mind from nature—namely the power of intentional concentrated attention withdrawing itself from the external world of matter. Through this sundering, this radical dualism, the lawful possibility appeared of a third force from a higher level (which he called "God"), reconciling and harmonizing the two realities of mind and matter. And such a state of affairs would eventually invite the question of man's true place in nature. Through an inner discipline transcending the mechanism of nature as it is, the great question arose: Was man's true function the enabling of the Earth to host a so-to-say God-infused materiality in the bosom of Earth, thereby helping the Earth to fulfill its own cosmic purpose?

I was stunned by the question. Could it be that the light of this great idea was waiting to be discovered in all the great thinkers that have shaped the modern world?

There, piled up on my desk, "seated" and leaning against each other on the once clear table surface behind me, was the honored company: Hegel, with his vast vision of the world-spirit unfolding the entire history of humanity; Immanuel Kant, proving that the human mind can ask but never answer the deepest questions about God, nature or reality. There, seated next to Kant, was Plato, the fountain-source of nearly every philosophical idea that has existed on half of the Earth for over two thousand years—along with Plato's own teacher, Socrates, dramatizing how great ideas and proofs, like the universe of suns, stars and galax-ies, emanate as immense effusions from the energy of human dialogue. There also was Aristotle, the engines of whose mind and powers of observation, empathizing with all of living reality, also swept the world, exposing and filling the spaces left by his teacher Plato.

But the philosopher I actually reached for was the great nineteenth-century Danish writer Søren Kierkegaard. I could almost say it was simply my hand that reached for Kierkegaard, even despite the fact that my mind was at the

same time slowly telling me that I should try my new method
of reading with one of the more academically "established"
philosophers that I have just mentioned—Plato, Aristotle,
Kant, etc. . . .

Reaching for Kierkegaard was like reaching for a stick
of dynamite. I remembered the explosion he ignited in my
mind when I first read, or tried to read, his book with the
startling title, *Fear and Trembling.*[16] Or another of his
books, also with an arresting title, *Concluding Unscientific Postscript.*[17] I remembered how these books at one and
the same time both defeated and inseminated my mind.
What was he saying? What was he doing? Yes—tearing
down the massive intellectual synthesis of Germanic metaphysics and philosophical speculation; yes, tearing down
mental explanations not only of Christianity, but of human life itself.

And yet—and this was probably why my hand reached
for him—and yet not a page, not a line, not a word about
nature or Earth or the universe. Of all the philosophers I
had read, there was none so apparently barren of thought
about nature, wondrous nature, wondrous stars and
worlds. Why then was I reaching for him? What could he
say that was at all relevant to the question of the meaning
of the Earth? It was that challenge that moved my hand
toward him.

I took in my arms the books of Kierkegaard that had

been my constant companion so many years ago—all with magnetic titles: *Fear and Trembling, Concluding Unscientific Postscript, The Sickness Unto Death, The Concept of Dread, Repetition,* and *Either/Or.* Carefully, lovingly, I made space for them next to the armchair in my office.

And happily went to bed, anticipating the freshness of morning when I would reawaken my passion for Kierkegaard and test my faith that his extraordinary insight about the human mind and soul had much to teach us about the Earth, even though I did not remember the word "earth" even once appearing in the books of his that I had so passionately read.

Elias was nowhere in my mind, and had been nowhere for weeks.

Chapter Thirteen

Crossing the Threshold

B ut that night, after long absence, Elias appeared.

Once again I am walking slowly toward the low stone wall. But this time Elias is already there.

Again, I could not at first make out the features of his face. He stood up as I approached and, without waiting for me to come closer, he said something I could not hear, the meaning of which, however, I understood. It was something like, "Come with me."

Immediately, it started to rain in the dream. When we were children, whenever it started to rain we would always go to his house. And so it was now, except that although it was raining in the dream neither of us was getting wet. He led me across Seventh Street.

We quickly came to his big, shining yellow house. It

was exactly as I remembered it, except that in the dream there were many more steps leading up to the ornately carved front door. As we walked up the steps, his face came into focus. He seemed even older than the last time he had appeared, his dark eyes even stronger, deeper, darker; his full-sail forehead wide and calm, his ears more prominent.

ELIAS HAD NO EARLOBES. And for some reason this feature had always fascinated me. On one memorable occasion he had noticed me staring at his ears while we spoke, and when I made some remark about them, he explained to me that it had to do with the fact that he was prematurely born. The earlobes, he said, are one of the last things to form in the human fetus.

This fact—if fact it was—had riveted me and provoked all kinds of questions in me. I remember being dumbstruck by the thought that this living person, my friend Elias, was a sort of substance, like a clay figurine that could be added to in increments and that, had he stayed longer in his mother's womb, a little more substance would have been stuck onto him. At the same time, he was *Elias,* the individual person. Was that also a substance that could be added to or taken away in gradual increments?

By then, it was already obvious that Elias was really

seriously ill. And I was now going almost every day after school to see him at his house instead of at the stone wall. On one particular day, looking at his ears and wondering about his illness, something like the following came to me: He was born too soon and he may die too soon. But what was *he*? Was *he* something that was dipped in a wrong way in the river of time?—the river of existence on this Earth? And what did *he* have to do with time? I remember thinking with my twelve-year-old mind: Yes, everything in nature, everything that lives, must die. But was *he, Elias,* just part of nature and nothing more? Yes, his body was sick, his body might soon die. But was he, Elias, a body? Or was he something else that happened to be *in* a body? Where did *he* come from? Where was *he, Elias,* going? And what of *me*? What am I? Where did *I* come from? Where am *I* going?

Several weeks later, Elias matter-of-factly told me the diagnosis was leukemia. And during the days and weeks that followed, the subject of death, his own death, came up many times. I was unsettled by how calmly he regarded it, almost as though he were simply looking forward to a new and interesting kind of experience.

In Elias's house there was what they called a music room, a wide sunken porch enclosed on three sides by windows with cream-colored velvet curtains tied back to let in the afternoon sun. In the center of the room was a long, slender, blond harpsichord and beside it a music stand with a straight-backed, armless chair placed in front of it. In one corner was a cello covered with a silk shawl to protect it from the sun.

The room was at the back of the house, just off the elegant parlor, and looked out over a lovingly tended garden. A chaise had been set up where Elias could lie back and read and look out at the garden. I would lift the heavy straight-backed chair from behind the music stand and carry it next to the chaise. I remember that during our talks I had to squint against the sun streaming through the wall of windows.

The day, I remember, was Monday. I arrived as usual just after school. Mrs. Barkhordian, a beautiful woman with enormous dark eyes and long, jet-black hair, briskly ushered me to the back of the house and then brought in a tray loaded down with a pot of fragrant tea, a plateful of homemade cookies, and a bowl filled with pieces of loukoum and foil-wrapped hard candies. And, also as usual, she stood there looking right at me and didn't leave us until she saw me take something from the tray and put it in my mouth.

I began by telling Elias about a show I had seen over the weekend at the Fels Planetarium, "The Origin of the Planets." I was surprised that he didn't seem interested—especially as this was a favorite subject of ours and we were both inordinately fond of the planetarium. But I went on talking. Elias seemed to grow restless. Finally, he interrupted me rather sharply.

"I've been reading up on leukemia," he said. My heart contracted as I listened to him explaining with cool precision how the production of normal red cells in the bone marrow is displaced by the production of lymphosarcoma cells. At first, I didn't want to hear any of that. But as Elias went on speaking about the physiology of the blood, I became more and more fascinated by the subject itself and was soon no longer even thinking about the fact that it was he, Elias, who would soon be dying from this, at that time, incurable disease. I was just sitting there gobbling cookies and discussing the functions of the various types of blood cells.

Suddenly, I saw tears coming out of his eyes and running down his cheeks. He fell silent and turned his head away from me, toward the garden. I also became silent. I thought that perhaps he was in pain and I started to get up to call his mother. Then he turned his head back toward me. Squinting into the sun, I saw that his whole face seemed to have gotten bigger and looser, as though it were melting. In a startling deep voice that came from far down in his chest, he shouted, "I'll never be able to *learn* about everything!"

The strangely powerful sound of his voice went right through me. Fighting back my own tears, I heard myself saying, also in an abnormally deep voice, "I'll learn for both of us!"

Elias looked at me as though I were a fool. In the same loud, deep voice, he said, "How do you know? Maybe you'll die soon, too!"

My whole body shivered. I no longer felt sorry for Elias. I, too, was going to die someday. An extraordinary vibration appeared inside me. I felt solid as a rock; at the same time the awareness of my own eventual death poured through me and terrified me.

We remained looking at each other for what seemed a very long time. We were equals.

I broke the silence. "Even if you weren't going to die," I said, "even if you lived to be a hundred, do you think you would ever solve the mystery of death?"

Elias turned his head toward the ceiling. He seemed calm again. His voice became soft. "Maybe," he said.

BACK IN THE DREAM NOW, Elias opened the ornately carved door to his house and ushered me in. Mrs. Barkhordian, Elias's mother, young and beautiful as I remembered her, was there busying herself as though nothing unusual was happening. She was preparing a tray with a teapot, cookies and candies. Once, she looked up without even acknowledging us, not even seeing us, or so it seemed to me. I made a move to go over toward her, but Elias, standing next to me, gently restrained me. "She understands," he whispered. "She knows what is happening. You mustn't disturb her." His face was full of joy as he looked at her. His eyes were glistening. It was the first time I had seen him like that in these dreams.

Again he said, this time in an audible whisper, "Come with me."

He gently took me by the arm and guided me through the elegant parlor. We stopped for a moment at the threshold of the music room. Standing there, I felt my breathing change. My chest started heaving. At first I didn't dare to look into the room and then when I did, the sunlight streaming through the wall of windows blinded me. I started to step back, but Elias gripped my arm and held me firmly in place. He urged me, nearly pushing me, across the threshold and as I started to step down into the music room, the sunlight softened and I was able to see clearly what was there. My whole body stiffened and I let out a little cry as I backed away. There lying back in the chaise was the young Elias. And sitting beside him was me, the young Jerry.

I started to wake up—I even remember my eyes several times fluttering open for a second, seeing the gray morning light filtering through the blinds in my bedroom. But Elias would not let me wake up. He gripped my arm tightly, painfully, and drew me back into the dream. Then he let go of me. And he stepped over the threshold down into the music room. "Come with me," he whispered.

I took the step down into the room.

I watched Elias, carefully averting my eyes from the young Jerry. Elias walked to the chaise and stood for a moment close beside the young Elias. He beckoned me to come forward and stand next to the young Jerry, who was seated in the armless, straight-backed chair.

As I did, I sensed the weight of my body, something I would have thought impossible in a dream. I sensed the weight as intense, intense weight, intense gravity. A heavy lightness—I can't say it otherwise. As I slowly stepped toward the chaise, following Elias's indications, I felt this strange sense of gravity growing stronger, as though I were walking on the surface of another world, another Earth.

We reached the chaise. I was standing next to the dream Elias and before me was the exact scene from my childhood. The young Jerry sitting in the armless chair and the young Elias lying in the chaise. Both the young Elias and the young Jerry, me, myself, were carrying on a soundless conversation, completely unaware that we were standing there watching them.

I couldn't bear to look at the young Jerry. I kept my eyes fixed on Elias standing at the other side of the chaise. Elias stood there motionless for what seemed like a long time.

I started to float upward, but Elias looked at me fiercely and the pull of the new gravity brought me immediately back down to the carpet.

Then I heard the young Elias speaking and at that very moment the old Elias, now once again in a gentle, tender whisper, said to me, "Do as I do." He paused. "Do it now."

I saw the old Elias enter the body of the young Elias and, as for me, with just the slightest impulse of intention, I entered the body of the young Jerry.

Suddenly, in the dream, I saw the face of the young Elias grow larger and more relaxed, and I heard him speaking in a deep, strong voice, and I heard myself responding, also in a deep, strong voice.

Exactly as it happened in the past, the young Elias was now saying, "I'll never be able to *learn* about everything!" And also exactly as I remembered it, I responded in an unusual voice, "I'll learn for both of us."

But now, here, in the dream, the young Elias did not look at me as though I were a fool, as had actually happened in the past. On the contrary. He looked at me soberly and peacefully. A long dream-silence followed.

I felt deeply quiet, deeply interested, deeply present in the body of the young Jerry. I did not want to be anywhere but there in the dream, in the body of my young self.

Finally, the young Elias said to me, in the same resonant voice, "It's happening, Jerry, isn't it?"

"Yes," I answered.

"And now it's up to you."

I wanted to say, "What? What is up to me?"

I woke up.

Chapter Fourteen

Man Is Not Yet a Self

O f course, I thought to myself, sitting at my desk in the early morning following the dream. Of course: What was Kierkegaard saying on every page, every sentence of his inspired writings? For man, he was saying, inwardness is all. Man's uniqueness consists in his capacity to turn his attention to himself, his capacity to turn his attention to itself and dive deeper and deeper into the ocean of individual human consciousness. He was born to choose that work, that free movement of self-discovery. Self-birthing. Only human beings are called to that.

I had awakened from the dream in a kind of quiet frenzy, with a sense of overflowing thoughts not only in my mind, but throughout my body: a sensation that my thoughts were coming from my quiet, compact body, compact in that

I felt everything in me pulled toward a center like an independent world being formed, like a moon forming around a planet, or a planet around a sun, or . . . ? I even felt the atmosphere around me charged with a fine energy—volatile, life-giving energy, and perhaps even a little dangerous. The thoughts flowed and flowed, but the body, moving through my house, was somehow at the same time still as a mountain.

Going straight to my desk, methodically, without hurrying, I somehow allowed my thoughts to tumble as much as they wished and I wrote down on a notepad what little I could catch of them.

- Man the microcosm, the micro-universe, the inner micro-God (the Self) emanating worlds within worlds.
- All of nature calling to man *to be*.
- St. Paul, Romans 8: "For the earnest expectation of the creature waiteth for the manifestation of the sons of God." "For we know that the whole creation groaneth and travaileth in pain together until now."
- Earth needs man to awaken, to live, to grow inwardly, to be.
- The future of the Earth is up to man. But first man must become Man (a son of God) in order

to manifest, in order to be able to do what only Man can do.

- Just as I must become my Self in order to do what only the Self can do: namely, to understand objective truth, to will objective good, to love objectively, consciously.

- Otherwise I, little man, little self, sows ever more the pain of meaninglessness and confusion.

- It is in my body, my Earth, that the Self needs to be born. That is, the body of the Self.

- Otherwise, more and more pain to Mother Earth.

I picked up one of the books of Kierkegaard and turned to the *one sentence* in all of his writings that had always confounded me and which at the same time seemed to be the key to everything he wished to say. Over the years each time that I found that my understanding of this sentence had grown, I also felt something new in it that I could not fathom. And so it was now, sitting at my desk that morning, after that dream. And what I was now seeing was the kind of thing I had observed just a few days before when calling up my recollections of Descartes. That is, I was observing how reading Kierkegaard affected not just my

thinking or my emotions, but my very state of consciousness. I can describe it in one compact expression: What I
saw while reading Kierkegaard is that the growth of real
understanding consists not in the discovery of an answer,
but in the experience of a question, and not just a new
question with a new intellectual content, but a new *kind* of
question, leading to a new *kind* of questioning. Not just a
new thought, but *a new part of the mind itself.* A new part
of oneself.

Here is the sentence—or, rather, the sentences. Every
student of Kierkegaard knows them and every student of
Kierkegaard is attracted and baffled by them. They occur
on the very first page of the book entitled *The Sickness
Unto Death:*[18]

> Man is spirit. But what is spirit? Spirit is the self.
> But what is the self? The self is a relation which
> relates itself to its own self, or it is that in the re-
> lation [which accounts for it] that the relation
> relates itself to its own self; the self is not the
> relation but [consists in the fact] that the rela-
> tion relates itself to its own self. Man is a syn-
> thesis of the infinite and the finite, of the
> temporal and the eternal, of freedom and neces-
> sity, in short it is a synthesis. A synthesis is a

relation between two factors. So regarded, man
is not yet a self.

I stared at these words, blackened as they were by underlin-
ing and a big question mark penciled in the margin.

And went for another of his books, using the same hand
that, by its own apparent self-will, had reached for the first
one. This second book had always been for me the sister
stick of dynamite: *The Concept of Dread*.[19] And sure enough, the hand opened this second book to pages that
shouted at me, almost derisively, about how wrong I had
been to think that Kierkegaard did not write about the
Earth. To be sure, the actual word here was "earthly." And
surely this was not the same thing as "Earth." Was it?
"Earthly" was some kind of ordinary religious idea, rather
uninteresting and certainly in no way related in any signifi-
cant sense to the Earth as a planet, as nature. Wasn't that
so? I could really ignore it. . . . Couldn't I?

And so, turning away from the word "earthly," I went
back to the mysterious paragraph on the first page of *The
Sickness Unto Death,* and its blazing, blinding, shining last
sentence, "So regarded, man is not yet a self."

Suddenly, a new thought appeared in me—perhaps
because I couldn't really shake off the radiations of the
word "earthly." That word, "earthly," evokes in me and

in many of us the idea that our life on Earth is only one part of our full life—or is meant to be only one part. It evokes the idea—wrapped as it is by now in cliché-ridden inertia—that there is also an aspect of human life that is not of the Earth.

I couldn't shake off this association. And so I tried to return to the mysterious sentence, the mysterious phrase, "not yet a self."

I called to mind—or rather, my mind was calling my attention to my own fundamental response to this mysterious paragraph, the fundamental response that always had governed my thoughts about it. And that fundamental response to that paragraph was to ask myself the question: "How then to become a genuine self?" How to repair this fundamental incapacity that Kierkegaard is speaking of? Over the years I had learned to carry just this question as the defining problem of human life, a problem that explained so much about my own life and the life of man on Earth.

But I now realized that this phrase had actually over the years decayed in my mind. From being a life-giving question, it had gradually and imperceptibly turned into a more and more deadening problem, recognized—if only in words—by nearly every psychological and neo-spiritual movement that comes down the road. It seems that everyone, everywhere, is being offered ways to "become yourself."

Suddenly, I was now realizing—thinking, but not thinking only in my head—that this situation of man is not something to be repaired; it is not exactly a problem to be solved. It is a state of consciousness to be lived.

I could not solve it with my mind and yet my mind was now glowing with calm light. And perhaps man cannot solve it in his life. Perhaps it is not meant to be solved—even though, and maybe especially though, one yearns to solve it, one yearns to answer this question.

But what about this "earthly"? I hadn't wanted to find that word, to see that word in Kierkegaard. I had wanted to test my belief that great philosophical thought by itself would point me to what is unique in man, would show me what is man's unique place on Earth. I specifically was not seeking explicit thoughts about Earth, neither religious thoughts nor scientific thought. I was looking for something about man that was much subtler, much deeper than theories about man. I was looking for something pointing, hinting, at something most real and most inexpressible about the human being in order then to ponder more deeply man's relationship to the Earth, what the Earth actually needs from us.

And now, as it always happened when reading this baffling paragraph of Kierkegaard, my attention was finally drawn to something in it that had always been even more incomprehensible, but which I had simply ignored until now. Something I always had carefully turned away from after deciding, long ago, that it was either a clumsy translation of the original text, or something that Kierkegaard had purposefully wished to make obscure. And yet each time I passed by it, I, so to say, in a whisper said to myself that I needed to understand it, that I would someday need to get off the train at this little local station with the mysterious name, and really explore this quaint village:

> *"The self is a relation which relates itself to its own self, or it is that in the relation [which accounts for it] that the relation relates itself to its own self."*

What can that possibly mean: "a relation which relates itself to its own self"? I could accept, in a pinch, that one might clumsily speak about a relation between two elements by saying that the relation relates the two elements. But what could it possibly mean that the relation relates itself to its own self? Isn't this a kind of gibberish? And then, as if that were not confusing enough, what of that little phrase in brackets? The translator must have had a reason for putting it there. It must be an essential part of the meaning. But what could it all mean? What could it mean to say, to summarize, that man is spirit, spirit is the self, the self is a relation (a synthesis) between Heaven and Earth (the infinite and the finite, time and eternity, freedom and necessity) and that this relationship relates itself to its own self, and that there is something or other about this relation that accounts for (or causes?) this relation to relate itself to itself? No wonder I never stopped to think about this paragraph! Why should I? Why shouldn't I just go on ignoring it?—especially since so much of the rest of the book, and so much of Kierkegaard's other writing, was deep and clear and offered one of the most profound visions that I have ever encountered of what a human being is!

Fine. Fine and good. But no, not so fine and good! What about that last sentence of Kierkegaard's, that last razor thrust: "So regarded, man is not yet a self"! How could I now just move on? There is no way we can understand our relationship to the Earth unless we understand what man is who inhabits this Earth, and what man is not: what man is and what he is meant to be. There is no way we can understand the Earth unless we understand man. And in order to understand and study man, obviously we have to understand and study ourselves, myself. Just as physics has discovered that it cannot study matter without studying the observer, that it cannot understand the laws of the physical world without awareness of the nature and influence of the observer—just so, we cannot understand the Earth without studying ourselves. We can't just dissociate ourselves from the Earth and at the same time out of the other corner of our mind say that we must include man—that is, human consciousness—as an organic part of the Earth, obeying the same laws that govern the Earth and its life.

We are children of the Earth. What is it about the Earth that brought us forth? That brought forth man with his human consciousness? How could we possibly turn away from that obvious question, so blindingly obvious that it is a wonder of the world that we haven't made it the heart and center of all our study of our planet—including our subatomic particles and metals and bacteria and mountains and climate and . . .

And please, please don't say that we have understood the place of man—that man is nothing but the most recent happy accident of mechanical, chance, random mutations provoked by the handy gamma rays bumping into the wormy chromosomes that make us what we are. No normal man, woman or child can really take that seriously unless they have inhaled the drug of scientism. Face it: We do not know what or who we are. And, now, with Earth and nature at the brink, we can no longer live without understanding the Earth, and we cannot understand the Earth without understanding man, and we cannot understand man without understanding ourselves.

At the same time, like all of life and like the planet Earth itself, we are also children of the Sun. Father Sun, Mother Earth. If the Earth is alive, then the Sun must also be, if anything, even more alive. We need to stop in ourselves. We need to ponder this notion that the Sun is also alive. It will lead us far beyond scientism and far beyond poeticism, fabulism, far beyond the madness of what we call objectivity and the madness of what we call imagination.

Chapter Fifteen

The Two Mysteries

I s it now the moment for us to present ourselves quietly and humbly to the good-minded scientists of our culture and present our dream, our vision in the form of a new question—or rather an old question coming from a new part of our mind? Is it time to ask the good-minded scientist this question—the Earth is a living organism, isn't it? Isn't that now acceptable? Gaia is no longer mere metaphor, isn't that so?

The good-minded scientist, and the good-minded scientific philosopher, without arrogance, listening to us, taking us seriously, replies that one of the chief defining characteristics of a living organism is that it reproduces itself. By that standard, he or she will tell us, we cannot really say that the Earth is an organism. Yes, wonders take place on the Earth, in nature, in the universe. And yes, life is a mystery, he tells us. But a mystery is made up of many small wonders, smaller questions that we can begin to untangle and explain. Set aside, for a moment, the big mystery and tend to the small phenomena in all their intricacy. Here, slowly, step by step, the mystery can begin to yield.

But here also is the good mind of our deeply respected pragmatist and down-to-earth American philosopher, William James, calling a century ago on the vision of the nineteenth-century experimental psychologist Gustav Fechner. Long before our contemporary concept of Gaia, the now practically unknown Fechner was offering this astonishing vision of the Earth. Here is a small fragment of what James so admires:[20]

> Long ago the earth was called an animal; but a planet is a higher class of being than either man or animal; not only quantitatively greater, like a vaster and more awkward whale or elephant, but a being whose enormous size requires an altogether different form of life. . . . What need has she of arms, with nothing to reach for? Of a neck, with no head to carry? Of eyes or nose when she finds her way through space without either, and has millions of eyes of all her animals to guide their movements on her surface,

and all their noses to smell the flowers that grow? For, as we are ourselves a part of the earth, so our organs are her organs. She is, as it were, eye and ear over her whole extent—all that we see and hear in separation she sees and hears at once. She brings forth living beings of countless kinds upon her surface, and their multitudinous conscious relations with each other she takes up into her higher and more general conscious life. . . .

Fechner likens our individual persons on the earth unto so many sense organs of the earth's soul. We add to its perceptive life so long as our own life lasts. It absorbs our perceptions, just as they occur, into its larger sphere of knowledge and combines them with other data there.

I HAVE ALWAYS longed for thought of such profundity. I have longed to face the questions of the heart with science in one hand and the spiritual quest in the other hand. Here is both the question of the miracle of nature, the mystery of the Earth and the Sun and the starry worlds; and on the other hand, the mystery of man, of myself, of what I am, of God in myself and in nature and the universe. In one hand sacred fact, sacred freedom of the mind to bring facts together into good-minded theory. And in the other hand the penetration of heart-insight, essence-questioning.

It was always so at the low stone wall when Elias and I were pouring out facts and more facts, theories and ideas wrought from good-minded science—and at the same time gathering into ourselves the sense of wonder, humility, the yearning to know and to serve something far greater than ourselves.

This is the gift of a scientist like Vernadsky who, just by stating the facts as they are known about the Earth and life and nature—just by presenting them with both his mind and his heart alive—offers the hope of unity between the mystery of nature and the mystery of consciousness, my own consciousness.

And, without naming it: the mystery of God. We felt, we children, without naming it or even knowing there must be a name for it—we felt the question of the relation between God, myself (man) and nature, the Earth. Yes— between human consciousness with its divine aspects of love, will and understanding—and on other hand, nature, matter, the Earth.

How could one find the real relation between conscious-ness and the Earth? Between man and nature?

But having the question in this form was already a

joyous event, an event filled with scientific knowledge and spiritual consciousness at one and the same moment— perhaps contradicting each other, but yet belonging to each other in the same unsolved equation.

And here was Kierkegaard and the bafflement of the relation that relates itself to itself. Here was Kierkegaard speaking at the beginning of his treatise about the all-pervasive human tragedy which he calls "despair." Despair, he tells us, is the fundamental anguish of specifically human consciousness. In the midst of his inspired serpentine logic, in the midst of his passionate, brokenhearted clarity, and after a hundred readings by a callow youth and an aging man, a simple truth shines through: The human being cannot become a self except by freely yearning to relate Heaven and Earth within himself, and in so doing rooting himself in the Power which created his specifically human freedom as so defined.

For, finally, to complete the picture, here is the one part of Kierkegaard's baffling paragraphs that both the young adolescent and the present philosopher have until now simply held in abeyance—while deeply respecting the depth of Kierkegaard's thought, never really understanding his full definition of what a human being is meant to be, that is to say, his definition of a human being who is free of despair, his definition of a real self:

This then is the formula which describes the condition of the self when despair is completely eradicated: by relating itself to its own self and by willing to be itself *the self is grounded transparently in the Power which posited it.*[21]

In a word, we cannot be ourselves without at the same time rooting ourselves in God. We cannot be independent beings without depending entirely on a higher force that penetrates our specifically human consciousness—if we allow it, if we choose it. *And the more we choose it, the more it chooses us.* Otherwise, our entire life is self-deception, hiding from our humanity with no hope whatever of finding the meaning of our life on Earth—in a word, *despair* in one or another of its many forms.

But where is science in all this? Where is my beloved nature, sky full of stars, wondrous human body? Where is fact? Where is the planet Earth, the orb circling the sun, the life populating its surface and its atmosphere?

What has become of the question of the heart that asks: What is the purpose of our life on Earth? It is now no longer merely a conventional way of asking, "What is the meaning of our life?" We *must* add the Earth to this question. If man is more than an accidental appendage to organic life governed only by uncaused mechanical laws; and if man is a being who is meant to be a conscious self;

and if there is no blind chance spewing life forms into the intricate web of life; if all life is inherently interconnected, as we are increasingly discovering; if all this is so, it is the Earth itself that is begging us to become a self. And if this is so, we must—as any good-minded scientist must—we must ask nothing less than the question: What is the purpose of the Earth within its own sun-centered world?

If the Earth is alive, and if the Sun is alive, then the whole planetary world must also be alive. Does our world have its own world? Does the Earth have its own larger world? And are human selves needed not only by the Earth, but by . . . the universe?

Scientist, can we now speak of God?

Chapter Sixteen

The Real Reconciliation

The following morning I swept all the philosophy books from my desk and replaced them with scientific studies of nature and the earth. This is probably what I would have written if this book were a work of fiction. But here at just this point the literal truth is of commanding significance and is evidence of how under certain conditions, especially when we are struggling with a deeply meaningful and intractable question, the events of our lives show the direction we need to take.

The following morning there appeared at my door the manuscript of a new book, *How to Build a Habitable Planet*, sent to me at my request by the author, a friend, Dr. Charles Langmuir, who is one of the world's leading earth scientists. In fact, he is the son of the physicist David

Langmuir, who was chiefly responsible for translating the great book of Vernadsky.

In an earlier conversation with him I learned that he had never actually seen his father's translation and I eagerly handed him the book. Looking through it for the first time, he pointed out that, of course, it contained assertions that needed to be corrected in the light of present-day geological science. That did not surprise or trouble me because it was not only the factual content of what Vernadsky wrote that touched me, it was its underlying sound of the immense unknown world that is our planet Earth, a "sound" that also evoked the sense of an unknown world in myself.

And now, by myself, I began to devour the contents of this manuscript that had been dropped on my doorstep. Even the tiniest glimpse of the immensity of scientific knowledge that now exists about the Earth; even the most elementary understanding of what is now known by astrophysics concerning the origins of the universe; or what is known by modern physics about the laws of matter and energy, including the ever-deepening paradoxical realities of the subatomic world; and including what is known about the chemical processes that created life on the surface of our world, and what is known about our planet itself as a great "fuel cell"; including what is known by paleontology concerning the fortunate catastrophes over billions of years that enabled the forces of emerging life to be nourished by the energy of sunlight—even this slight sensation of the vast weight of modern science—all this reminded me in my bones of my love, my childhood rapture in the world that science brings to light.

And there I am, as I read on and on—science in one hand, spiritual striving in the other hand. With an entirely new intensity of conviction, I feel it is necessary, it is urgent, *we are yearning,* to bring the two hands together.

Earth in one hand, Heaven in the other.

Matter and life.

Body and mind.

It is urgently necessary to find—not a premature, superficial "oneness," but *an objectively real duality*! We need, urgently, to make the correct separation in order to struggle toward the objectively real oneness, or synthesis—in our understanding and in the life we live.

It is not that duality in itself is wrong. But it is *the wrong duality* that haunts our minds and hearts and action in the world. If we can find the true duality, then at that moment we are already, by this very fact, at the doorstep of the right synthesis, the true oneness, the unity we are yearning for—in our understanding and in the life we live.

What is the real two-ness in the universe? Is it man the knower, and nature, the known? Is it the Creator (God) and the Creation (including man)? And what is the real dualism in man, in human nature, in ourselves? All great books, almost every new and exciting discovery by science, especially by earth science on the one hand and brain science on the other hand, converge on the question—the ancient eternally unanswered question: What is Man? What is the specificity of the human being? What is it that makes us human, uniquely human?

This purely scientific manuscript in my hands powerfully calls me into that question. The future of the Earth and the future of humanity depend on our understanding how to think about the question: What is Man? What *kind* of thought does this question demand of us? And is that last question itself—the question of what it means really to think—is that question itself the first clue to where, exactly, we will discover the true uniqueness of human nature and our task upon this Earth? What does it mean to think with the whole mind? What does it mean to *think like a man*?

In any case, the aim of my friend's book swept me more and more deeply into my childhood love of science—a love that caused me to regard scientific facts the way a monk regards holy scripture—taking it all with such passion that my logical mind was irrigated with the feeling one has in front of ancient symbols. I was not tempted to read spiritual interpretations into the facts and the theories so carefully presented in this new book. I didn't need to. Because once again I was a child—a child of five, a child of eight, of ten, of twelve, pouring my whole heart into the powers of my logical, analytic mind—recording facts and scientific theory as though they were the words of God-the-Universe.

Forgotten for now was all philosophy, all religious language, all theology, all metaphysics, all esoteric and mystical truths. I didn't need them.

Here before me in this excellent book, the planet Earth was going to be seen within the great scale of the universe and its unfathomable origins, the creation of starry worlds and galaxies and clouds of immeasurable energy, of elements forming, atoms and molecules coalescing. Our Earth itself, therefore, a world within the world of the Sun and the solar system. The world of our Sun and solar system itself within the world of our immense galaxy, the Milky Way, within which billions of other new worlds come into being and pass away within the scale of immeasurable time and space. And the world of our "mother" galaxy is itself a world within a world—what world? What world contains and nourishes galaxies? The universe itself as a world, the great world of the All and Absolute . . .

I pored over the list of chapter headings: the universe and its birth; galactic worlds and their birth; the synthesis (birth) of stars; the substance and energies of the sun; the formation (birth) of planets and moons from suns and nebulae (clouds of starry matter and energy) . . . and on and on . . .

And suddenly, my mind stops. Scanning the pages, the child in me nearly weeps as I read:

> If we consider life as a planetary process, rather than some separate phenomenon that occurs on a planetary surface, then planetary evolution includes all aspects of the planetary system— core, mantle, crust, ocean, atmosphere and life. Life plays a critical role in planetary evolution, by capturing and storing solar energy in planetary materials, modifying the oxidation states of near surface reservoirs, and influencing all layers of the Earth with which it comes into contact. *Life is in turn greatly influenced by the physical processes of planetary and solar system evolution.*[22]

I am thinking: It is all alive. It is all life: Man, Earth, Sun, stars. And what is life but directed movement? Movement that is not only *horizontal*, but also and stunningly *vertical*. That is to say: *evolution*. Directed movement upward and downward, toward and away from its timeless origin. Man within Earth, Earth within solar system, solar system within the radiant embrace that is the world of the Sun, the Sun within the galaxy, the galaxy within the . . . All.

Life within life. But more: *evolution within evolution.*
Organic life, nature, evolving within the evolving Earth.
The Earth evolving within the evolving world of the
Sun, the Sun evolving within the evolving world of the
galaxy . . .

Evolution within evolution.

But how? By blind chance? Impossible! But how else?
By the hand of God? Fine and good, but still—how? *How*
does God create? How does He think? Do we really need
Him in order to understand? Of course, yes.

And no. It can only be by not needing Him that we can
understand life. And, perhaps also, understand God.

I am thinking: Observe! Study! Think! Exist as a man,
the being who can think consciously. Abandon God in
order to be found by God.

Where did life come from? Where *within life* did Man
come from? No blind faith in either God or not-God.

"I make no hypotheses"—Isaac Newton, after charting
the universal laws of gravitational motion and energy.

The scientist looks and observes. We listen to him and
think with him. I plunge my mind into the living material
world. I make no hypotheses. I try to look with the eyes of
science. I try to observe what the scientist reports, and
I ponder what he honestly thinks and what he honestly resists thinking. He wants to be objective, impartial,
clean. He will resist calling on God and he will also resist

denying some form of directionality in the movements of life—biological life. And to biological life, we will add also planetary life, cosmic life. Evolution—the movement upward toward greater and greater wholeness and unity— that is to say, systemic complexity held together by systemic energy—otherwise known as mind. For what is mind but the lord of complexity, bringing oneness, unity, fertile emptiness into the thousand elements and beings within its radiance and influence?

It is all matter, materiality. Great ideas—what are they but representations of the deeds and sufferings of matter in all its gradations and levels? Consciousness—what is it but the formless throbbing of intentional materiality folding in upon itself under the hand of the eternal? Chance mutations of the DNA—the forces of chance directing matter to higher and higher levels of materiality. Chance—chance destroying its own creations in the death and disappearance of nonadaptive biological variation.

I am thinking: How naïve is our view of chance and necessity! As though it were a simple either/or. Are there not levels, *qualities*, of chance everywhere in life? Think, think! In everything and everywhere, reality exists at different levels of power, meaning and action. Therefore, there must be levels of chance as well. Levels—stages of development which require from the surrounding, enveloping worlds different levels of energy, different levels of nourishing energy—as the Hindus say, it is all food . . . everywhere and everything.

From what I am reading, it is clear to me that at each stage of what the scientist calls evolution, a new level of chance operates, a new kind or dimension of energy is received by the developing organism, be it plant, animal or planet.

I am now riveted by a narrative in this book pregnant with meaning, pregnant with mind, yet utterly material, physical, nondirectional—chance again and again flowering into choice on a cosmic, planetary, terrestrial scale. Who or what made a universe like this?—with chance and choice, randomness and design, coiled around each other like the two serpents of the caduceus. Two opposing yet intertwined movements. Contradiction at the heart of reality.

Out of nowhere, the "big bang," the cosmos begins. Out of nothing, even before space and time existed. Absurd. How can anyone in his right mind speak seriously of "the beginning" of time itself? The mind kicks like a wild horse. Does that mean there was time before time? Otherwise how could one even speak of a "beginning," which implies a point in time? And how can anyone in his right mind speak of the "appearance" of space itself, which implies a point surrounded by a vast, static nothingness—in other words, empty *space*? Yet scientists, brilliant and sober, with mature minds, speak like this, masking the absurdity with a second absurdity—"we do not know . . . *yet*." As though someday, by the same quality of reasoning and research, we will know how and when and where it all began! Ignoring the obvious truth, which is not known or felt with the whole mind: An absurdity at the heart of knowledge renders all that knowledge itself, if not absurd, at the very least temporary, relative, purely hypothetical.

And good scientists know this, they know that all our science is provisional. And yet the vast body of science grows and proliferates endlessly and brings about technological marvels that are seen as the marvels of our understanding.

And nowhere, never, is it felt that it is our instrument of knowing itself that is the mystery and the problem. Why is it not even suggested, even in a dream, that the very essence of our knowledge is in question—that we do not know with the whole mind, but only with a part of the mind? A part of the mind that willfully cuts itself off from our own inner universe, our own sun, our own inner sources of light and warmth and process. Our state of consciousness, our mere fragment of the whole mind, can never understand that which requires the whole mind to understand.

An absurdity at the heart of knowledge is like a cancer at the heart of a life. The life goes on in its way, but unknowingly racing toward its own premature death and destruction as the absurdity creeps into all the cells and tissues of the being . . .

And yet—the scientific narrative thrills even as it flattens our vision of our universe and our planet and life itself. The thrilling narrative takes us from the whole of the universe to the amazing birth of stars and galaxies, our own mother galaxy, the Milky Way, the swirling birth of our Sun with its life-giving energy pouring itself out into space, as do the countless billions of solar worlds throughout the universe, pouring their own sunlike energies into space, presenting the picture of the entire universe filling with who knows what kind or what *levels* of emanations and radiations capable of—and *created for?*—the insemination of the next order of worlds, planets so constructed as to host the interiorization of life-energy through the evolution of one-celled beings, microcosmoses, which themselves evolve and feed on the level of energy needed from the sun. And the whole drama of life on Earth beginning from the Sun and, yes, not without the influence—but at what level?—of energies from all the solar worlds, the radiations and emanations that fill the universe, perhaps existing at who knows what levels of life and energy. The Earth, shall we say, needs or feeds on certain levels of energy, certain food, at one stage; but as terrestrial life, as the whole living planet, evolves from its core to its outer atmosphere, the Earth needs different levels and qualities of celestial energy. And so we find the appearance of oxygenic photosynthesis, the release of the life-giving poison called oxygen which a new level of life—growing toward the animal—now needs.

The animal/plant/microbe, the atmosphere, biosphere, mantle/core—it all now needs a new level of chance, a new and finer level of radiations from the starry worlds and the Sun itself, a new food in order to make the next leap of being. And all the Earth conspires at the same time to keep the constant pulse of terrestrial life—rock yielding its chemistry to root, root softening and unlocking rock, soil and plant inseminating the air, air nourishing bacteria and the microbe, the microbe enriching the surface of the world, creatures in their meanest and greatest complexity—worm, centipede, beetle, spider, flying, crawling, curling, spiraling, swallowed by and swallowing the surface life—the plant world unfurling its albedo, its necessary protecting shade over the Earth to allow the warmth and the coolness to bring forth the animal life that will capture a new level of chance radiations that until now merely passed through the planet, but which now need to be held by the Earth as the new food for the new intentionality of the new life waiting to be born and to inhabit and to define the meaning of this world, this realm, this Earth.

Is this not the "esoteric" in broad daylight? Is this not mystical rationality? Is this not chance becoming choice?

Choice incarnating through chance? Fact becoming idea, idea incarnating into fact? Does this not feed the senses with truth? Does this not wrap tall garments of glory around "mere" fact? Does this kind of story not throw a vertical robe of inner conscious meaning across the horizontal, "god-less" parade of scientifically posited systems which have been named universe, galaxy, star, sun, planet and moon? A high vertical line thrown across an immeasurable horizontal stretch of space and time. The warp and woof of the web of life. Sacred fact! Empirical God! Spiritual body and celestial Earth.

THE HEIGHT AND BREADTH of Reality filled with meaning and direction. And at the same time, automatic. Lawful, mechanical.

Can I surrender to this noble contradiction? Can I give up the drive to prematurely resolve it, explain it? The temptation to reduce it to something that offers only a brittle unity, a shallow "answer" to an unfathomably deep question?

Isn't this what life is? Both organic life and my human life? Isn't this where man and nature, stone and mineral really meet—in the realm of an invisible reconciling energy that synthesizes two opposing forces?

Isn't this what Kierkegaard is teaching us about self-hood, mind, spirit?

We name it *evolution*. The name is itself a world, a cry for symbolic vision, synthesis, unity of oppositions.

Of course. In my ordinary state of consciousness, I am not able to reconcile oppositions, real oppositions, real contradictions, the real dualism.

Either in nature or in human life. The solutions, reconciliations and compromises we come to in our ordinary state of consciousness are fraudulent, masking one side or the other side, not really resolving or reconciling.

The real reconciliation is not an idea, a plan or an explanation. Not more information or more theory or borrowing half and half. The real reconciliation is going to be something totally new, totally mysterious—yes, a new birth, a new being, a new state of being, even. It is happening all around us—it is life itself at every level. What is defined by contradiction at our level is reconciled only at another level—not so much of thought or feeling alone, but of something quite new, quite other. Something that only a god can do, an angel, or God himself. Reality itself is a higher level than our little mind, our little life.

Chapter Seventeen

Earth, Man and the Brain

Like a great wave breaking and spreading out before us, the question "What is Man?" begins to enter anew into our modern world. Earth—Life—mineral, plant, animal—Man! But now, here, beginning to flow through the avenues of our culture, the ancient question takes its present form: the scientific study of consciousness and the human brain.

Earth science shows us the thick interrelationship between the planet and organic life, showing us that everything on Earth and the Earth itself is alive, showing us that the origin of life is life itself, the origin of the universe is the universe itself, and time and space are their own unfathomable origin. In these root questions and paradoxes, purpose and accident embrace each other. And just as the ancient question of the beginning and meaning of existence—this ancient question of God and Reality and Meaning—has in our time incarnated in the body of earth science and biological science, just so has the ancient and primordial question "What is Man?" incarnated in our time in the emerging field of neurological science, with all its attendant specializations of organic chemistry, genetics, computer science, systems theory, bio-engineering, robotics, etc.

These two great sciences—earth science and brain science—now represent, for our present era, the two great questions of nature and man, matter and mind—ancient, timeless questions wearing ancient garments of religion, myth, ritual, speculation—from even before ancient Greece, ancient Jerusalem, ancient India, China—from the sands and jungles of the old human and animate world. Just now—as man rises up to either heal or violate Mother Earth to an extent that his presence now defines an entirely new geological era, the *Anthropocene* era—just now the two great questions mix and fuse: planet Earth and the human brain.

We cannot understand Earth without understanding what the Earth has brought forth in Man—ourselves—and *why* it has brought forth Man—ourselves. Nor can we understand Man without understanding the extent to which the laws and forces composing the Earth govern our human nature. Like two great rivers converging, the scientific study of life on Earth is now blending, and needs to blend, both scientifically and metaphysically, with the study of the human brain.

Does this mean that modern science is about to confront one of the most essential questions of all human life: the relation between the outer world and the inner world, the two streams of universal energy that flow uniquely through man—uniquely, that is, in that within the human psyche they are meant to be inwardly harmonized in the embrace of the uniquely human intentional struggle to become a fully human Self? Just as the biological human child is born of the transcendent outward fusion of the two universal energies of sex, so the inner child—the fully human being—will be born from the inward harmoniza-tion (Kierkegaard's "synthesis") of two opposing universal forces—the inner world and the outer world, eternity and time, freedom and mechanicalness—Heaven and Earth.

Is brain science on the verge of achieving what many of the greatest minds of our era have sought to achieve: to introduce the uniquely inner life of man—inwardness—into the vast, vast bosom of rationalistic materialism that defines our era?

What is the Earth? Nature? What is Man? Conscious-ness?

What, or *who,* am I?

THE SKY WAS darkening and an audible wind was moving in the trees outside my window.

Pushing back from my desk, I closed my eyes, hoping to find some inner quiet.

But after a few minutes of trying to separate from my thoughts, I was drawn into an image from the depths of memory:

It was the summer of 1952, between high school and college, on the way, as I then thought, to a life in medicine and biological research. Through the intervention of a well-connected relative, I was working as a substitute autopsy assistant, or *Diener,* at the University of Pennsylvania Hospital in Philadelphia, preparing bodies for post-mortem examination. As I have described elsewhere,[23] my task was to prepare cadavers for the doctors and to help them while they performed the autopsies.

I was preparing two, and sometimes four, cadavers a day. At the same time I was reading every medical book I could get hold of. And from everything I understood in these medical texts, and from what I saw and sensed every day with my own eyes and felt in my own hands, and from everything I heard from the doctors who patiently answered all the questions I poured out to them, I found myself facing an intolerable contradiction. The human body, my human body, was so wondrously constructed, so unified, so resilient, so intelligently adapted to the world around it, that it was incredible it should ever die at all. But for the same reasons, it was equally incredible that it should continue to live more than a fraction of a second in a universe the basic makeup of whose unalive atoms and elements was so alien to it.

In short, day after day I was absorbed by the problem and the mystery of time—defined as the paradoxical fusion of being and nonexistence, life and death.

Particularly vivid is the memory of removing the brain.

It is now the first time that I am holding a human brain in my hands, my slippery, thinly gloved hands. My heart is pounding from my head to my legs. I quickly glance around the lab to make sure no one is about to come in and see me simply standing there doing nothing, motionless, staring at the brain in my hands.

How is it possible? How could the immensity of human thought come out of this wrinkled object? The immensity of human feeling? Love? Hate? Consciousness? World-striding action? How could this *thing* bring forth the glories of art and music and science and religion and civilization? Along with colossal horror, brutality and evil? How could it *know, understand*? How could it *be* as a human being *is*—so infinitely more than what it, this thing, *is*? What magic supernatural forces did it contain? Did it *once* contain, this brain, when it was living within the gray flesh stretched out on this long metal table? How could it have ever been *I am*?

And someday it could happen, *will* happen, my own body on such a table, my own brain, perhaps, in someone else's hands. But for now my own brain is receiving impressions of this other human brain outside of me. And at the same time, through a distinct movement of my attention, I am aware of my thoughts and feelings from inside myself. From inside my own brain.

Again I look. I pretend to study. I pretend to be surprised that I see no traces of thought or feelings or of Man's entire earthly identity scarred in the convoluted landscape of this once living brain. But would we, could we, see such traces if we could look inside the living human brain? If we could observe the cells and neurons of the thinking, feeling human brain? Because, seen from outside, as I am now seeing it, it is nothing but a mass of soft gray tissue.

It will be almost half a century before science begins to become able to look directly inside the physical, electrical, chemical processes of the living brain. And yet . . . and yet, science, neuroscience in all its unique glory of technology, remains locked outside the *mind* no matter how deeply it probes inside the brain.

And this is the necessity that now faces the scientific

exploration of the mind—the need to see the depths of the mind from inside as we develop more and more instruments for studying its housing, the brain, from outside. By itself, modern science, no matter what instruments are in its hands, will forever remain locked outside of the mind. Here, too, as with the gathering fate of science in the whole of our civilization, our knowledge outstrips our being. For to see the mind from inside requires an entirely different movement of attention, an inward movement of consciousness itself. Without that, without intentionally cultivating the uniquely human capacity of what Kierkegaard speaks of as *self relating to itself*, it will be with neuroscience—as it is in our time with all the sciences—a case of knowledge outpacing being: knowledge exceeding our moral power and our ability to *understand*.

Modern science knows only what the ancient traditions would call "appearances." Its power is also an appearance. Science "works" in that it manipulates the surfaces of reality. There is another knowledge that knows meanings, connections in all worlds. This is what is called *understanding*. Understanding works with realities that include and involve meanings.

But perhaps I am going too fast. For the moment, can we be content to say that our science deals with man as a creature living under the domination of natural law, the laws of earthly nature, the influences of the Earth? That is, after all, both the integrity and the limitation of science: that it conscientiously limits itself to studying the laws of the Earth alone—that is to say, the influences and forces that operate within what the ancients called the plane of the Earth—the so-called "flat earth," by which is meant the ontological level of the Earth, the level of being of the Earth. All of our science is a science of the Earth, no matter how far into outer space our instruments project us. Metaphysically, "vertically," scientific man cannot leave the Earth's "atmosphere," and never will unless in ourselves we learn to participate consciously in the influences emanating from different levels of energy and action in the universal world.

Chapter Eighteen

Beyond Nature

That night Elias returned.

But it is not the music room in Elias's house. Nor the low stone wall.

It is a completely different place, a different setting.

I am walking alongside a rippling, curving stream. Elias is walking next to me, the *young* Elias. In the dream, we have just come to a particular part of Philadelphia's Wissahickon Creek, after walking through a wild forested park, following the meanderings of this storied flow of bright water.

I become aware that inside the young Elias is the old Elias. In the dream, I can actually see the vague outlines of the older man under the smooth childhood face of my young friend. My dream-thoughts are something like this:

Elias will soon die and he will never become the older man who has been visiting me in these remarkable dreams. The older Elias is the future Elias, the future he was never given. But what is the dream telling me when I see that the younger Elias now in the dream has his future within his body?

In fact, I now see more and more of the older man within the boy. I begin to make out the lineaments of the body of the older Elias under the skin of the boy—as we walk together along the bank of the flowing water.

And more, much more: I see two hearts within him, side by side: one vibrant and red and the other seemingly made of yellow light. The sight of these two hearts causes me to cry out in the dream, "Elias! Elias!"

And suddenly, for a brief second, I am seeing the inside of his head, the inside of his brain. In that brief second I am filled with an extraordinary joy. There, inside his head, I see, for that brief instant, a vast night sky filled with countless stars.

I am stopped in my tracks. I start to speak, to ask him about what I have just seen, but he looks warmly at me with his young face and eyes, placing two fingers on his lips, calling for silence.

We continue walking. He leads us away from the water back into the forested park, but the sound of the rushing Wissahickon remains, as though we were still alongside it. The terrain begins to slope steeply upward and, as we climb side by side, a high floating bridge comes in and out of view.

Elias whispers something to me, but the sound of the creek obscures it.

"What did you say?" I ask.

Again he whispers. And again I cannot make out exactly what he is saying. Something about the true uniqueness of man.

"What did you say?" I repeat, anxiously.

He stops. The water grows louder, joined by the wind in the trees around us.

He turns toward me. I am looking at the great smooth sail of his forehead, trying to see inside him once more.

He looks at me, examining me, with the eyes of the older Elias. Moments pass with only the sound of the wind and rushing water.

"Later," he says softly.

Quietly, gently, I wake up.

THROUGHOUT THE DAY I could not let go of the image of the doubly young and old Elias speaking to me amid the densely packed trees along the banks of the Wissahickon Creek. I continued off and on to hear the last word he had spoken as the dream ended. "Later," he had said from within the sound of wind and water, as though the Earth itself were whispering to me.

Why? Why "later"? Was it only because I hadn't been able to hear him? But if so, why wouldn't he have simply spoken in a louder voice? But of course, it was only a dream obeying its own dream logic.

Wasn't it?

"Later" . . . "later": but then, when? How much "later"? And for what? What was I supposed to be waiting for?

The dream has stayed with me. But what has especially stayed with me, as the days have passed, is what I saw behind Elias's forehead: *a vast night sky filled with stars.*

And here is what I am now thinking—about our Earth and the uniqueness of Man—and about the new, present-day passion to study the human brain, which is to say the new, present-day passion to understand consciousness, to understand the self, to explain, within the strict confines of scientific method, the essential nature of our human-ness, our personal and collective identity, while yet holding fast to all the principles and canons of scientific knowledge—knowledge that is, first and foremost, knowledge of the Earth and its laws. Can science, which originally took its strength by rigorously excluding consciousness from the field of its investigation—can such science now understand the very element it initially ruled out as an object of study?

How can science, which was founded, and whose success was obtained, by excluding mind and meaning from the Earth, which was the primary object of its study—how can such science now understand meaning and purpose, which are the defining attributes of mind, selfhood and consciousness? How can such science now study and explain mind, selfhood and consciousness without, in the process of studying them, denying their essential attributes and leaving only the corpse of the mind, the dead body of consciousness, of selfhood—an abandoned world, drained of its specifically human element?

Has the scientific method finally encountered something *in nature* which fundamentally eludes its grasp?

By excluding the properties of mind—consciousness, intention—from the world it is studying, in order to be free of dogma and unverifiable speculation, hasn't science therefore excluded the mind as a possible object of study—no matter what it may discover about the brain?

Working from the outside, outside the object it is studying, we now know a very great deal about the Earth—its long planetary history, its chemistry, its forms of biological life, the history of its biological life. And everything we know, all the vastness of what we now know about matter and life and nature—all of that taken together exists under the umbrella of one great idea, one great vision: and the name of that vision is *evolution*. And this word, this idea, is meant not only to *fit into* the whole of our scientific knowledge; it is now meant to *encompass* it all, all that we know, all that we know through rigorously excluding the nonobservable, the invisible consciousness, mind, from our theories and explanations. If evolution is to be a science within which all of our science finds its place, then this over-arching vision will obey, even epitomize, the exclusion of consciousness and unverifiable purpose, unverifiable intentional directedness, from the object of its study. And we have gone very far with this understanding. We have amassed an immensity of knowledge seemingly about almost everything there is or can be. And we have faith that what we don't now understand, we will someday understand, little by little, by uncompromisingly adhering to the scientific method of thought, which, like an angel holding a flaming sword, keeps us away from believing that conscious purpose is at the heart of reality.

But now we come to Man and we wish to include Man under the umbrella of our rigorous science, rigorously excluding consciousness as an irreducible property of the object we are studying—even when we begin to speak of such things as "the wisdom of the body," or the biosphere as itself a vast living organism.

But now, here is evolution, the evolution, perhaps, of the Earth itself, its latest manifestation being the human animal, mankind, humanity.

The paradox is clearly stated: How can we dream of including man, uniquely the being who has mind, selfhood and consciousness, under the umbrella of a science that in principle refuses to admit the irreducible existence of mind, selfhood and consciousness in the object of its study? How can Man be seen as occupying a stage of evolution if the process of evolution in principle excludes the essence of Man?

That is the contradiction that haunts the brave attempt in our modern world to bring the scientific method to the study of the mind and heart of man.

THE POINT IS not that the laws of biological evolution contradict the laws of consciousness. Rather, what needs to be seen is that a different level or world begins just where biological evolution leaves off. We may speak of outer evolution and inner evolution—the former obeying scientifically perceived and studied laws of nature and the Earth; and the latter an interior process of evolution in which other laws begin to operate, laws having to do with capacities and energies that are unknowable by ordinary sense perception and the instruments and technologies that are the extensions of what we identify as the five senses. On Earth, inner evolution takes place uniquely in man and depends on elements uniquely defined by the type of words used by Kierkegaard: inwardness, self relating to itself—or, rather, *that in the relationship which, grounded in the eternal, relates the self to itself*—and thereby brings forward into human life, *into the human body*, what the great teachings call the Self—in other words, the *soul*. And in order for this process of inner evolution to begin, what is required is the sustained activation of capacities not yet, if ever, measurable by the science of our era: capacities such as truly conscious attention; genuine freedom or creativity; objective conscience; the genuine force of will; and impartial love.

Summing up these elements, we may speak of the evolution of man as the process by which human beings become able consciously and voluntarily to serve the purposes of higher, perhaps the highest, intentions in the universal world, intentions that create and maintain worlds upon worlds in the universal world. And here we may also boldly speak of *the intentions of the Earth*.

Chapter Nineteen

Why Is Man
on Earth?

"There are periods in the life of humanity, which generally coincide with the beginning of the fall of cultures and civilizations, when the masses irretrievably lose their reason and begin to destroy everything that has been created by centuries and millenniums of culture. Such periods of mass madness [often] coincide with geological cataclysms, climate changes, and similar phenomena of a planetary character . . ."

On one occasion when speaking of the orderly connectedness of everything in the universe, Gurdjieff dwelt on "organic life on earth."

"To ordinary knowledge," he said, "organic
life is a kind of accidental appendage violating
the integrity of a mechanical system. Ordinary
knowledge does not connect it with anything
and draws no conclusions from the fact of its
existence. But you should already understand
that there is nothing accidental or unnecessary
in nature and that there can be nothing; everything has a definite function; everything serves
a definite purpose. Thus organic life is an indispensable link in the chain of the worlds which
cannot exist without it just as it cannot exist
without them. It has been said before that
organic life transmits planetary influences of
various kinds to the earth. . . . The earth . . . is
growing; not in the sense of size but in the sense
of greater consciousness, greater receptivity.
The planetary influences which were sufficient
for her at one period of her existence become
insufficient, she needs the reception of finer
influences. To receive finer influences, a finer,
more sensitive apparatus is necessary. Organic
life, therefore, has to evolve, to adapt itself to
the needs of the planets and the earth. . . . The
evolving part of organic life is humanity. . . . If
humanity does not evolve it means that the

evolution of organic life will stop.... At the same time if humanity ceases to evolve it becomes useless from the point of view of the aims for which it was created and as such it may be destroyed. In this way the cessation of evolution may mean the destruction of humanity.[*]

These words were spoken a hundred years ago in Czarist Russia on the eve of the Russian Revolution and under the gathering storm of all-consuming global war. Very soon there would be little doubt that the whole of modern civilization was in mortal crisis. Yet it would still be many years until there was even a hint that nature itself, the Earth itself, might be at risk. With the prescience that characterized so much of his teaching, Gurdjieff situated the emerging crisis of our era within a cosmic, planetary context.

The Earth, he taught, needed not only man, but awakened man. Humanity in general had appeared on Earth partly through the same biological laws of evolution that had brought forth and sustained organic life millions of years before. But other laws and cosmic influences also operated in the arising and destiny of humanity. Man's

---

* G. I. Gurdjieff, in *In Search of the Miraculous* by P. D. Ouspensky. New York: Harcourt, Brace, 1949, pp. 305–306.

unique structure, and the fundamental reason for his appearance on Earth, lay in his possibility to transcend the broad biological laws and mechanisms that governed the rest of organic life: Human evolution crucially depended on the inner world of man himself, on his own voluntary inner efforts. While remaining deeply enmeshed in and subjected to the interconnectedness of organic life on Earth, the human being also possessed the capacity to go beyond the biological laws of organic life and develop in himself a state of conscious selfhood. Where other forms of life reach their completion and serve their function fully governed by the laws of nature and the Earth, Man, the unfinished animal, was uniquely endowed with the capacity and the *responsibility* to absorb and respond directly to conscious influences from *above the level of the Earth and the Sun.*

Without man, these higher influences could not pass into the life of the Earth. And without receiving these influences, the Earth herself could not evolve toward her own greater possibility. But nothing in the universe stands still. Everything from stones to stars is in movement, either toward or away from its uniquely possible completion. It therefore follows that without absorbing these higher influences, from "above the sun," the Earth, in the words cited earlier, "will fall down," perhaps in the sense adumbrated by the geochemist Charles Langmuir, who directs our attention to the state of the dry, perhaps lifeless planets in our own solar system, such as the planet Venus. The Earth, perhaps, was once like that many millions of years ago. Without humanity serving the function for which it appeared on Earth, our own world could revert to the status of the same relatively barren world it once was in the profundity of the remote past.

SUCH IDEAS, when I first came across them as a young man, both chilled and enthralled me. Already, at the start of my academic career in philosophy, I had become acquainted with the visions of man and the cosmos offered by many of the world's spiritual traditions, but I had never come across anything quite like the cosmological ideas of Gurdjieff.

In order to explain why these ideas had such an impact, and why I believe they are of immense importance in the crisis of our era, I need to retrace some steps.

The truth is that at first, in those early years as a professor of philosophy, I never took the cosmological doctrines of traditional religion or ancient philosophy as anything more than inspired speculation. Deep down, I grimly accepted that the scientific picture of the universe was the literal truth—the picture of the universe as a vast dead sea with consciousness and purpose residing only in the lonely vessel of mankind, a wandering speck of meaning adrift in a meaningless universe.

It wasn't that my childhood love of nature and science had now vanished. Not at all—that love had lost none of its intensity. But it had retreated and protected itself behind the wall of scientific authority that has defined our culture's main interpretation of reality. I confined my love of nature to my own subjective world. I joined the existentialist philosophers who resigned themselves to a godless, dead universe while powerfully asserting the primacy of man's inner freedom and powers of intellectual and artistic imagination—like a proud but anguished cry that made no echo.

I all but forgot that in my childhood I was able to love the Earth and the sky all the more as I studied science. I felt no contradiction in sensing the universe of science as a greater consciousness than my own—although at that age I never knew much about that word, "consciousness." But in the passage of time I forgot the low stone wall and how Elias and I would often bring ourselves to the verge of tears merely by citing facts and numbers and scientific accounts of how all things on Earth and above the Earth worked together not so much like a great impersonal machine, but, in the treasured statement of Sir James Jeans, like a great thought.[24]

Elias, friend of my mind, friend of my heart, how could I have forgotten?

Elias and I never really spoke about religion, although

the idea of God always entered into our talk. In fact, we really knew practically nothing about religion except what I experienced under the hand of orthodox Jewish grandparents, and what he experienced within his Orthodox Christian Armenian family. It never entered our minds that religion had something, anything at all, to say about the world of nature, or about planets, stars, galaxies, or about the immense reaches of space and the mysteries of time.

And so as I grew into adulthood I relinquished to science the right to think seriously about nature and the universe, and I restricted my search for intimate, living truth to the region within the fortress of my individual mind, individual man "thrown," in the words of Martin Heidegger, into the heartless spaces of scientific reality. In this act of relinquishing, I was of course submitting to the whole philosophic current of the modern world. The exclusive right of science to know what is the Earth and the universe had been at first sharply resisted by religion, but eventually religion had limply and quietly surrendered that right to science.

But to repeat: Within that fortress of the lonely mind there was a community of rebels with whom I instantly bonded—Kierkegaard, Nietzsche, the existentialists, the poets and artists—who refused to be colonized by the worldview of science. Huddling behind stony walls, we rebels implicitly granted to scientism the vision of a meaningless universe, while passionately cultivating the soil of our own cosmically anomalous human consciousness.

At the same time, I eventually, gradually, began to take more seriously ancient views of the universe that were a fundamental element of the spiritual traditions of mankind—this without in any way challenging the unquestionable sovereignty of science in matters of real fact. It was actually quite easy to take that turn. Fact was one thing—and science had the just claim to fact, to literal truth. But metaphysical vision was quite another realm and could exist side by side with scientific fact as long as metaphysics staked no claim to the scientific hegemony—that is, to the literal truth about nature and reality. Philosophy, metaphysics, was fine and good—if kept within the fortress, of course. We were tolerated, we even received friendly visits from time to time from our scientific masters. But we had to stay in our places.

It would be years before I came to realize that genuine metaphysical knowledge was knowledge at a different level than scientific knowledge. It was years until I saw that the modern rejection of metaphysics and esoteric cosmology was nothing more nor less than the rejection of higher levels of consciousness. The general worldview of modernity rejects the existence of higher levels of being, higher levels of reality which are invisible to the sense-based knowledge offered by science. In rejecting, in not seeing the possibility of higher consciousness in man, science was also blind to the existence of higher, deeper levels of laws and purpose in the physical universe. It could not see the existence of both higher man and higher Earth. There is an invisible man, the possibility of whose existence haunts science, just as there is an invisible Earth that haunts our scientific knowledge of nature and our planet. This higher knowledge, this higher man, this invisible Earth does not contradict anything truly discovered by sense-based knowledge. On the contrary, invisible man includes visible man; invisible Earth includes visible Earth.

We cannot truly understand either man or Earth without access to all levels of knowledge, perception and being. But of course there also exist imitation metaphysics and purely fanciful attempts to transcend the rigorous demands of scientific standards of knowledge. And there exists metaphysics which is only theoretical and mental. Scientific knowledge rightly rejects what it sees as pretensions to so-called "higher knowledge." But when science assumes that it itself is the only kind or level of true knowledge that can exist, and when it insists that physical man, as we know him, is the only kind of human being that can exist, then at that moment science decays into scientism.

Modern science itself does not know that there exists another level of knowing that is as genuine and precise as science itself is and wishes to remain. Not recognizing that such genuine higher knowledge is possible and does exist, it cannot discriminate between incomplete or imitation metaphysical knowledge of nature and genuine expressions of higher consciousness, higher knowledge. It cannot know the invisible Earth that lives within and around the visible Earth, just as it cannot know the invisible man that can live and does live within visible man. And perhaps—perhaps—just as invisible man is yearning to enter the actual life of visible man, so also invisible Earth is striving to enter the life of visible nature, visible Earth. And, to some extent at least, the very arising of human life on the Earth is the expression of the yearnings of invisible Earth.

For myself, in my own life, a profound change of attitude toward traditional cosmology began with my study of Plato. Yes, so I thought, perhaps Plato's view of the cosmos was only high speculation, but however that may have been, I began to see in Plato's view of the universe something utterly compelling. For Plato, ultimate reality is not the unconscious, indifferent play of blind forces of the modern view of the world, under which, in the words of Bertrand Russell, "man is the product of causes which had no prevision of the end they were achieving," laws and forces under which "his origin, his growth, his hopes and

fears, his loves and his beliefs, are but the outcome of accidental collocations of atoms," and under which "no fire, no
heroism, no intensity of thought and feeling, can preserve
an individual life beyond the grave," and under which "all
the labours of the ages, all the devotion, all the inspiration,
all the noonday brightness of human genius, are destined
to extinction in the vast death of the solar system," and,
finally, under which, "the whole temple of Man's achieve-
ment must inevitably be buried beneath the debris of a universe in ruins."[25]

Not so for Plato. On the contrary, for Plato value, meaning and purpose were written into the very essence of reality. He spoke of ultimate reality as "the idea of the Good,"
by which he meant that existence itself, being itself, is at its
core the manifestation of pure, timeless goodness, pure
timeless beauty—thin words, perhaps, but which yet represented, in abstract form, the super-intensity of the essence
of reality. And this doctrine Plato carried into his teaching
about the essential meaning of human life. For Plato there
could be no real knowledge of nature and the Earth without the personal cultivation at the same time of the inner
state of human being called *virtue,* another word that has
now become thin and meager, and even somewhat quaint.

For most of his life, Plato rooted the main elements of
his philosophy in his dramatized figure of Socrates who,
in his face-to-face dialogues with those who approached

him, treated all fundamental questions of knowledge as requiring the individual human being to bring his attention inward, to the work of developing his own soul, his own inner essential Self. There could be no knowledge without virtue, just as in the universe there could be nothing existing without the forces of justice and goodness infused in matter and nature. The basic import of this revolutionary doctrine of Plato about the fundamental identity of knowledge and virtue has been so misunderstood and so far forgotten that it has sometimes become, where it is noticed at all, even the butt of mockery in the intellectual mainstream of our culture. What is no longer understood is that Plato spoke of virtue as both a cosmic reality and a psychological state of being in which the deepest capacities of the human mind, heart and body are harmoniously interconnected in order to perform their fundamental functions of knowing, caring and doing.[26]

I cannot say that I had more than a fleeting glimpse of this deeper meaning of Plato's vision, especially as he presented it in his later works, and especially in the majestic dialogue called *Timaeus*.[27] For over a thousand years, this dialogue was an immense influence on the mind and worldview of Western civilization. There Plato reveals precise elements of his vision of the universe and the Earth as manifestations in the realm of space and time of that absolute invisible and timeless reality which we would now call

God. As a young philosopher, I only touched the edges of his notion of cosmic reality and all of existence as expressions of timeless, value-laden essences. But even at the edges of his vision, I found myself taking more seriously the teachings about the universe and about nature and the Earth in all the spiritual traditions of mankind. I began to understand how Plato's vision, together with the tough-minded and all-encompassing genius of his great pupil Aristotle, also provided much of the conceptual structure and language of the Judaeo-Christian worldview. And I began, dimly, but deeply, to sense that the superpower of modern science was actually a branch of the very spiritual vision of reality that its agnostic and atheistic representatives so vehemently opposed! What a sublime irony!

In what became the Judaeo-Christian worldview of Western civilization, ancient Greek rationality blended with the symbolic, mythic narrative of the Bible. In the womb of that specific view of the universe, of man and the Earth, science itself in both its ancient and contemporary forms was nourished and given birth. Our science itself, with all its rigorous resistance to seeing intelligence and purpose in nature, is actually, fundamentally, *a child of the Judaeo-Christian religion*—in which the whole of reality is seen as immersed in the purposes of God.

In the words of one outstanding scholar, the book of Genesis tells us that

. . . the world, in spite of its imposing appearance as a self-sufficient network of interconnections and causal laws, is a mystery hanging in the void. Whatever we can explain—and it is quite a lot—by definition only refers to relations *within* the world. The world as a whole remains mysterious . . . [but ultimately] it is God who is mysterious and the world is his creation. Man as a bio-physical organism is part of creation; but he is also more than that. . . . In spite of his organic unity with creation there is also a distance, a chasm which separates the two. Man as a biological organism is immersed in the world, but he also confronts it in his consciousness, his conscience, his capacity for abstraction and language. To nature, that is, creation in the "raw" state, he opposes culture—creation transformed and perfected.

The human response to the world is twofold. Like other animals, man is an integral and dependent part (or victim) of nature. But unlike the animals, he is actively and creatively responsive. He beholds the world and forms mental images, ideas and abstract concepts of it. The Greeks called this *theoria*. He also consciously and purposefully interferes with nature. To this

end he, as it were, transcends nature by artifi-
cially prolonging his hands: he fashions tools
for himself and becomes *homo faber* [man the
maker]. In Biblical language all this would simply be expressed by saying that man is a link
in the order of creation, that he was created
together with the other animals on the sixth
day, but that he also has in him the divine spirit.
Created in the "image of God," he conceives of
the specifically human quality in himself, of
that which sets him apart, over and above the
rest of creation, as his divine likeness. He is, in
fact, a miniature God. Within his human limits
he creates, like God. . . . By working, by creating culture out of nature, man truly emanci-
pates himself from his natural state. He is no
longer victimized by nature, nor blindly preying
upon it; but in his hands, like primeval chaos in
the hands of God, nature becomes a raw material to be fashioned according to an idea and a
purpose.[28]

Thus when scientism denies purpose in the cosmos it is
nothing less than man himself denying his very own essential being.

Without knowing all the far-reaching implications of

this clarification of the cosmology of Western civilization, I no longer was intimidated by scientism and felt free to allow my childhood love of science itself to expand even more and to read the book of science as a sacred text just as the medieval era read the book of nature. But it would be many years before that wish of the child, now reborn in the adult, was able to be realized in practice in the details of everyday life.

As for the cosmologies in the religions of Asia, I have already described how, as a young professor of philosophy, I appreciated them without actually feeling *the shock of truth* from them, in myself and about myself. How far I was from experiencing the Hindu and Buddhist visions of the universe as both metaphysical and psychological at one and the same time! Didn't the traditions of India speak always and everywhere of the cosmos as permeated by the supreme consciousness called Brahman and Atman? Yes, and I loved that idea, but it was impossible and even inconceivable that it applied to me, personally—inconceivable that it had anything to do with my own life as I actually lived it. So much was this the case that I was not even aware that its practical application was for me unimaginable.

And it was the same with the traditions of Buddhism that so appealed to me. I was deeply intrigued by the central Buddhist teaching that the self was an illusion, but I was not able to fit the elaborate and gorgeous cosmological ideas of Tibetan Buddhism into the same mental space as that central teaching about the self. So it also was with Zen Buddhism and its profound sensitivity to nature and the life of the Earth: the impressions of the silent awakening of Buddha-nature in its visual representations of water, wind, bird, flower and branch—as well as what nature and Earth really were in the transcendent emptiness of its haiku poetry or in the steadiness of hand in its sublimely minimalist works of craft with fired earthen clay and simple carvings of living wood.

Only much later did I begin to *experience* that it was not only about myself and my own life, but also and even more fundamentally about the Earth—our, mankind's, cosmic home.

But the young professor of philosophy was confronted by something in myself of quite another kind in Gurdjieff's teaching about the Earth and the universe. And, along with that inner "taste" of something uniquely real within my own psyche, I began to intuit something also of quite another kind in reality itself, in the universe itself, in our Earth, in life itself in all its manifestations—something I had only dreamed about or deeply, deeply hoped for and sensed as a child looking up at the night sky or into the eyes of an animal or a human being or, at rare moments, at a simple stone. I began to have moments when I sensed that existence itself was the mystery, being itself was the mystery. It was a mystery that anything should exist at all; and that whatever does exist incarnates and obeys an unknown active energy which I longed to understand.

I will try to say more about this now, although it will be obvious that only a special mastery of language or art can do justice to the task of representing the energy and the laws of being. Such language and such art have existed throughout history, a language and an art that have the power to evoke in us the fleeting taste of the higher consciousness that created them, a glimpse that points unmistakably toward the Source itself of Being. Such art is sacred art in the most rigorous sense of the word. But even more fundamentally, men and women have also existed throughout history who in greater or lesser degree consciously incarnated the laws of the energy of Being in their presence and in their action in the world.

When I was a young academic beginning to appreciate the cosmological philosophies and mythologies of other epochs and peoples, I certainly never dreamed that they were describing *facts*. In my mind there was a wall between facts and values, between pure brute existence and purposeful intelligence, creative love, struggle and will. On one side of the wall was neutral, value-free scientific fact, the real world. On the other side of the wall was imaginative beauty and profundity of ideas, meaning, purpose. I loved and admired each side of the wall, the realm of fact on the one side and the realm of meaning on the other side. On the one side of the wall, the realm of fact, the human being lived, breathed, bathed in a meaningless ocean of factual realities, chemical elements, ions, tissues, food. Materiality. Brute matter obeying merciless laws of physics. On the other side of the wall, mortal man had to create his own great meaning through philosophy, spirituality, literature, music, art, moral action, adventure, human love.

I never dreamed that there was no wall—because, as the cosmology of the Gurdjieff teaching showed, the wall existed only as perceived in the state of human consciousness that he called "waking sleep." For awakened man, man as he was meant to be, there were two great movements of energy, one movement flowing down from the Source of the universe and another majestic movement flowing and struggling back toward the Source, the proto-cosmic and pre-cosmic unity. Awakened man could lead and did lead a life in which a conscious third movement, energy or force harmonized and supported each of the others in the greater conscious life. In this conscious life of awakened man the *conscious third force* engendered a life above biology, a life both within and above the Earth.

The third force of life existed always and everywhere, from the merest cell and the merest inhabitant of the sub-atomic world to the great dynamic movement of cosmic entities existing at vast levels of purpose beyond our imagining. This mysterious harmonic interdependence of the two movements of energy away from and toward the Source was the deep meaning of life itself, always and everywhere, from the minutest symbionts of intracellular organic entities to the great animate life on Earth and among worlds and suns and galaxies and cosmic entities even as yet undiscovered or imagined. And these two movements were given names that immediately broke down the wall between fact and value, immediately broke down the wall that separated brute scientific reality and conscious, intelligent purpose and meaning. The names were *evolution* and *involution*.

The mystery of living things, animate beings, consisted in the inextricable harmonization of two opposing forces—opposing in that they moved in opposite directions, *involution* away from the Source and *evolution* toward the Source. Under the invisible (to us) influence of the third energy a being lived its life, the glow of life permeated its existence and was felt by a child looking at it in wonder, or by a man of science or a philosopher or a poet, artist, builder, yearning to understand.

But this yearning, this yearning to know, to understand, that so many of us feel as young children, and as we become adults and seek to find our way in the rough and tumble of everyday life—what is this yearning, really? This need, this inner impulse which Plato called *eros*, love—love of truth, even love of Being, love of the Good? What is it, really?

Of course, I had no real name for this yearning as I sat with Elias at the low stone wall. Our culture calls it the love of knowledge, the wish for knowledge. And Aristotle famously said, as did his teacher Plato, that all men by nature desire to understand—in their essential being. But what was it really? The culture gave it a name, even sometimes calling it—borrowing the name from the ancient master, Pythagoras—the love of wisdom, not simply the love of knowledge. But again, what was this element called "wisdom"?

And how was it so intimately connected to the sense of wonder in front of nature, Earth and the vastness of the universe? Here the ancient cosmologies stare at us, stared at me in the face. As I began to respect them as great creative poetry, as great fundamentally deep human legends, as symbolic realities, as truth of a sort—but not as fact— even as I welcomed their mysterious beauty, their thrilling power to see, perhaps even to see me, to see, that is, to explain the mystery and the sorrows of human life—even then they stood outside of me, these ancient cosmologies, even as the cosmology of modern science stood outside of me. Perhaps the ancient cosmologies were true poetically and the modern cosmology was true factually—still, both were somehow outside of me; or rather, I was outside of them. Neither ancient meaning nor modern fact was about . . . about . . . *me, myself, my own eyes, my own fragile and mortal selfhood.*

Both science and ancient teachings were fundamentally alien to my most intimate sense of identity. Wonder in front of living beings, wonder under the vast sky, wonder at the structure of the atom, the mathematics of homeostatic metabolism within the human body and within the innards of the breathing Gaia that is our biosphere—it was still outside of me, outside of my, so to say, *I-ness*. And I did not know they were outside of me! I did not know it! I believed and felt they were my interests, that they, science and myth, had to do with my deepest wishes. Yes, that was true, but so relatively true, so true only just under the surface of oneself—both for me and for our culture, our modern humanity.

No! I, we, all of us, were still alienated from reality, no matter how excited we felt, interested in our science or our literature or our art or our ethics. We still yearned, driven by an *eros* we didn't understand and whose name we didn't know. For a period, for a brief period, the scientific revolution brought the beginning sparks of the shock of truth, but the fire it lit soon took up as its fuel the all-too-human desires for comfort and pleasure and invention and safety, power, and, finally, humanly decadent strivings of hatred, self-importance. . . . Yes, science brought material good of many honorable kinds, but it failed eventually to warm our inner lives with that which is the real aim, the real intention of the sense of wonder and the yearning for knowledge. All the benefits that science brought, and they were many, somehow, in ways we didn't understand at all, took us away from that primal yearning, *took us away from that in ourselves which was the root of that primal yearning.*

And here is where the ideas of Gurdjieff did not just look at me, but entered into me in a way that made me sense that something was involved that was entirely different both from what I loved as the science of nature and what I deeply respected as the ancient teachings about man and the universe. Something entirely different was involved which yet embraced them both and seemed somehow to preserve them both in an embrace that placed them as two essential aspects, or levels, of a greater whole.

Here was the answer to the question that I didn't know needed an answer—the love of knowledge, what was it? The yearning for wisdom, what was it? My precious talks with the young Elias—what were we searching for as we plunged into the discoveries and questions about the Earth, the sun and the stars and the plants and the animals and our own human bodies and our own lives and our eventual, all-too-soon deaths? What did mankind itself yearn for in that bright stripe of human history to which we give the name of the quest for knowledge, the yearning to be one with nature, to live with the sources of life that we feel and sense in the natural world of the Earth?

As I read and studied the ideas of Gurdjieff I was repeatedly stopped in my tracks by the idea of the possible states of human consciousness. And I soon realized, at first dimly and elusively, that what I longed for as a child and as an adult and—as it became clear—what mankind longed for under the names of wisdom and knowledge, was consciousness! What I longed for was consciousness. What mankind longs for, whether we know it or not, is what Gurdjieff spoke of as the state of consciousness that is our birthright as human beings.

And this is what the planet Earth needs from us. This is the missing element in our understanding of why man is on Earth.

Chapter Twenty

The Hope of the Earth

I s it really so? Is mankind's yearning for knowledge and understanding actually the yearning for consciousness? Is that what the Earth uniquely needs from us?

I remember the astonishment I felt when I first heard this idea about the Earth coming from the remarkable Jeanne de Salzmann. That was years ago, and by then I had already become well acquainted with the vast range of the ideas of G. I. Gurdjieff and with important elements of the inner work that was the practical core of his teaching. Although, as I have already said, I did not then know how this idea about the Earth was to be understood, I remember the immediate flash of joy I felt on hearing that this teaching had been brought to the world to serve a great universal purpose. The teaching was not just about *me*. It was for the

Earth itself and in some essential way for the universe itself. That feeling, however, instantly flowed into the shock of truth about myself: the truth of my own inadequacy, my own smallness. But this shock of truth was not what is called a "negative emotion." On the contrary. This sense of my own smallness was so deep and sure that it brought, as I now see so clearly, a strange and powerful current of hope.

Even then, after so many years studying this teaching, I had no words for the feeling of hope that this idea about the Earth brought. There was a mystery in this hope, a mystery somehow inextricably mingled with the truth about my own smallness, inadequacy, my own ignorance, my own lack of understanding. And not just my own smallness, but the smallness of humanity itself.

This is essential: It was truth itself, truth in its essential nature, truth in its greatness, its measure embodying the very Earth, the very cosmos, that brought this entirely new quality of hope. *Truth itself brings hope so long as it is the whole truth.* Truth brings objective hope even when that truth shows us things about ourselves that we can hardly bear. This strange new feeling of hope was in fact what initially brought me toward this teaching in the first place— this teaching that man, myself, humanity itself, is asleep, lost in illusion and fantasy, unconsciously obeying automatisms and influences that draw us outward, away from the source of the genuine selfhood which is our birthright. I am speaking of the hope brought by the fact that truth actually exists, and that there are people who are actually trying to bring such truth to the world.

WHAT I NOW SEE is that under the surface of my everyday self-image, there lies a deep correspondence between the Earth and myself, Earth and Self. My smallness—yes—was on the surface of my self, a surface that went, so to say, very deep; but my true identity, what Kierkegaard called "that in the relation which relates itself to itself under the eternal": My true identity was the Self. But here the language of Gurdjieff comes alive: My true identity is consciousness. I live my life on the surface of myself, and no matter how far I burrow into that surface, no matter how deeply I go with my mental logic and information and personal emotion, I can never discover the Source of my being—just as science as we know it can never discover the meaning of the Earth in the universe.

It is meaning itself that is hidden from us.

But in order to understand such expressions, it is necessary to have personal experience of the state of consciousness that is our birthright, which defines us as human, as Man.

This state of consciousness in its many levels is what has

been spoken of in all the great spiritual traditions of the world. In the Judaic mystical tradition it is the experience of *neshama,* the higher soul; it is the Christian experience of the inner Christ; the Hindu experience of *samadhi*; the Buddhist experience of *satori* and *nirvana*. And in all these traditions there now exist men and women seeking to bring the meaning of such experiences into the contemporary, threatened world we live in. They are seeking to bring these experiences of man's higher nature from the ancient world into the modern world; or from the Eastern world into the Western world. These representatives of the ancient spiritual traditions of mankind, including our own Native American teachings—they are all telling us that it is not just a matter of our personal development, not even that our modern civilization is at risk, but that the whole of mankind's survival, and the life of Earth itself, is at stake.

But inevitably the efforts of these representatives of the ancient teachings are being met by the overwhelming forces of modernity, beginning with technology in its accelerating deconstruction of all the patterns of living that have guided humanity through the ages—in the meaning and the content of knowledge, memory, power, love, communication, the education of children, relations between old and young, between parent and child; deconstruction of the quality of friendship, community; deconstruction of the primal human capacity for music, art, the use of the hands and muscles of

the body; even of the ancient limitations of space and loca-
tion that have acted to define the body of our physical and
social lives.

And all this is happening while leaving untouched and
often even intensifying mankind's ancient hatreds and
prejudices and deeply rooted impulses of self-love, vanity,
violent reactivity, addiction to empty pleasure, lethal sug-
gestibility, immersion in an atmosphere of lies in almost
every scale of activity: from the flood—in biblical propor-
tions—of information tainted by disguised opinion and
egoistic agendas, to the decay of ethics in commerce, gov-
ernment, science and human relationship.

It is true that countless small, private acts of compassion
and tenderness, heroism and sacrifice, the capillaries of
human goodness, continue to find their way into the human
mass that is our modern culture. But the hope for contemporary humanity that these small, private acts continually
evoke ultimately beats its wings in vain. The human mass
itself remains so saturated with fear and self-deception that
the sum of individual initiatives of genuine moral action,
creative intelligence and religious feeling seems continually
to be overpowered and deflected by the collective forgetting of mankind's true Self.

One may say that the world has always been this way
and has always been so understood by spiritual teachers
and guides since the most ancient times. But the unique

form taken by this perennial human predicament in the inner and outer conditions of our contemporary world is making modern man more and more incapable of sensing the shock of truth that these ancient teachings originally brought to the world.

What has become of faith, love and hope, one or another of which elements define the root strategy of almost all of the ancient spiritual paths now struggling to bring help to our modern world? What is really at the heart of these ideals and qualities that define the true being of man and no doubt his true purpose on Earth?

What is the root of faith, love and hope? What kind of power is real human power? What kind of strength is genuine human strength? What kind of love is the love that unceasingly gives of itself as it opens to the universal energies of compassion and justice and mercy? And finally, what kind of body is the true human body? How does it grow? What is its nourishment? What is it meant to become? Why was the physical body born so weak, so naked, so blazing with a possible future struggle for light and warmth and imperishability?

What is Man?

What is Consciousness?

Chapter Twenty-One

What Is Consciousness?

The question of the meaning of the Earth leads inescapably to the question of consciousness. And to ask—What is consciousness? is to ask—What is Man?—because beyond all biological aspects and evidence, it is specifically human consciousness more than anything else that defines the uniqueness of the human species.

Could we ever hope to understand our planet without understanding why we have been brought forth on the Earth? Without understanding all that Earth needs from us? It cannot be merely to correct the ecological problems we have ourselves created. There must be another function for our unique species, our specifically human consciousness. So much is obvious. There is nothing purely accidental in nature, nothing that is not implicated in the wholeness of the living world.

Therefore, the burgeoning scientific study of consciousness actually represents an indispensable element in our study of nature and the Earth. We can no longer separate the study of nature from the study of man, the study of consciousness. Therefore modern science, despite originally denying consciousness, purpose and meaning as properties of nature, was sooner or later compelled to bring consciousness into the center of its enterprise. Ultimately, there can be no science of biology, no science of ecology without a true science of psychology. Nor, therefore, can there be a complete science of physics and chemistry without a fundamental linkage to the understanding of consciousness. Science itself needs to be inclusive of all of nature or it is not science at all; it is only an accumulation of fragmentary information and unstable theories devoid of meaning. For if there is something fundamental in nature that, in principle, it can never really explain— if there is some primal element of reality that it assumes it can never acknowledge and *experience* as real—then it means that there is no part of reality it will ever truly understand.

A world is a unity. All of reality is everywhere entangled in everything. And the study of this unity must itself be a unity. That has always been the great wish of science—to understand the laws that govern everything there is in nature. And nature includes Man. And Man is consciousness.

Therefore, the science of consciousness is inescapable.

And many people believe that this science has now arrived. That it is here—appearing everywhere under such names as neuroscience with its many branches such as neuropsychology, neurobiology, neurotechnology, neuroethics, neuroeconomics . . .

But in this far-reaching, burgeoning field of consciousness research there needs to be recognized a large invisible element in human consciousness comparable in its importance to the dark matter and dark energy that we are told comprises all but a small percentage of the known universe.

What is this invisible element, without recognizing which we can never understand consciousness and therefore never understand the unknown world that is man and the Earth and the universe itself?

IT IS NOT EASY to characterize what that invisible element in human consciousness is, save to say that it has to do first with the role of feeling. We are speaking here of an inquiry that might be called "inner empiricism," as contrasted with the sense-based "external empiricism" that is the bedrock of the scientific method. That is, we are speaking of knowledge also rooted in direct observation, but in this case observation of the *inner* world of man, *requiring a specific preparation of the inner world of the observer himself.*

Throughout all of human history the great cosmological teachings that decisively influenced the development of entire civilizations have been deeply infused with this, to us, invisible element. All of mankind's fundamental visions of the Earth and the universe have emerged from within traditions and methods of living that are meant to transform the level of human consciousness, including the function of feeling. Or, to say the same thing, that are meant ultimately to provide access to an energy that transforms the whole of the human organism, inescapably including feeling along with the intellect and the instinctive and motor functions that bring about action in the world.

To speak more precisely about this invisible element, it is necessary to draw a distinction between two aspects of the human psyche, a distinction that is not recognized in science or in the worldview of our scientifically conditioned modern civilization. These two aspects may be called *feeling* and *emotion*. In our ordinary thought and experience, these two words point to one general class of functions and reactions—love, hate, sadness, pity, resentment, compassion, fear, delight, etc., etc. But, as a general rule, in the inner practices that lie at the heart of the spiritual traditions, many of these reactions and impulses are recognized as egoistic and are understood as a fundamentally unnatural and unworthy element of human nature. In addition, and this point is obvious to any honest observer, these egoistic reactions and impulses are of little worth with respect to the attainment of knowledge. Our usual emotions are notoriously biased and, in a negative sense, subjective. Their main function of evoking psychological pleasure and pain serves as a motivating force in our lives, but in themselves they do not bring us objective knowledge either of our selves or of the external world.

Our modern scientific ideal of objectivity requires that we try to separate our attention from the dominating influence that ordinary emotion exerts upon our perception and thought. But in this task of freeing oneself from the self-centered emotions in order to obtain objective knowledge, science has unknowingly prevented itself from seeing the function of genuine feeling hidden behind emotion. This quality of genuine feeling is in fact indispensable in acquiring objective, impartial knowledge of the real world both outside of oneself and within one's self.

Without the sustained development of the function of genuine feeling, the objectivity which science offers is therefore both humanly superficial and empty of meaning.

Real truth, real objectivity, is never superficial, never empty of meaning, never cold, never disconnected from an overall sense of the living Whole and the higher purposes within the Whole. Knowledge that comes only from the operation of the isolated intellectual function brings neither warmth nor light: neither the warmth of meaning nor the light of understanding. The impartiality which it settles for is actually a kind of mirage, based as it is on the activity of merely *one part* of the whole human mind, namely, thought disconnected from feeling. *Impartial* knowledge requires the activity of *all parts* of the human mind, each part contributing its specific energy and quality of perception. That is the very definition of the word "impartial": that is, knowledge that is not partial, not the product of only one part of the whole human mind.

The human body also must play its fundamental role in the attainment of knowledge, and everything that needs to be said about the invisible element of real feeling needs also to be said about the unique contribution of sensation. But it will be enough now to concentrate on the role of feeling, if only because the role of the physical body in sense perception is of course well known, being one of the main pillars of modern science as the ultimate test and authority upon which theory is based. That the human body's capacity of sense perception, while representing the strength and firmness of science, actually represents only the mere surface of the human body's possible contribution to objective knowledge need not detain us for the moment. It is the hidden element of feeling that is most important now.

And it is most important because even here, in the realm of genuine feeling, we are still not at the root, not in sight of the *level* of feeling that nourished the ancient teachings about nature and the cosmos—and which nourished the ancient teachings about human consciousness itself.

As HAS BEEN SAID, spiritual practice, in its many forms and in its many variations of sequence and emphasis, generally seeks to free man from the level of consciousness in which egoistic emotion dominates our lives. But spiritual practice also inescapably involves the persistent, continuing cultivation and refinement of *authentic feeling* as a necessary element of its work, the inner work leading to the awakening of the Self.

Such authentic feeling—non-egoistic feeling—is known to every normal person. The sense of wonder before nature, wonder not yet mixed with the desire to *do* anything with the wordless knowledge it brings, is one such common feeling that is unmixed with self-love. Like many children, Elias and I bathed ourselves in the sense of wonder translated into the authentic love of knowledge for its own sake, the yearning for understanding that is actually an aspect of the yearning for consciousness of the Self. But this motivating energy of the love of knowledge, which is actually the yearning for consciousness, is easily deflected or absorbed by mental and emotional associations involving action in the external world—in a word, technology. And what modern technology ultimately serves, honorable as it may often be in its original aims, is the part of the human mind that seeks safety, self-love, comfort, power, recognition, wealth, etc. The love of knowledge, which is actually the yearning for Being, may be present in the individual scientist, but it is almost always hijacked by the aims and purposes of a culture in which humanity is increasingly at the mercy, inwardly and outwardly, of elements which have no interest in the development of consciousness.

The love of knowledge, which is actually the yearning for consciousness, and which almost all of us vividly remember from our childhood, is in fact a taste of experiential knowledge brought by non-egoistic feeling. Many scientists as well as many artists and poets treasure this form of non-egoistic feeling throughout their life and work.

But precious as this quality of feeling is, it is still not in itself the invisible element of feeling at the root of the objective knowledge of nature in the teachings of the ancient traditions. What, then, is this invisible element of feeling that plays such an essential role in the attainment of objective knowledge? From all that has so far been said, one thing should be clear. The invisible element of feeling we are speaking of involves a certain personal struggle with one-self, a certain level of inner sacrifice, suffering of a kind that is also largely unknown, invisible, in our general culture.

Just as there is a quality of experiential *knowing* that is unknown in our modern worldview (a knowing that is carelessly and superficially labeled "mystical"), so there is an unknown quality of suffering and sacrifice that is also profoundly unknown in our daily life and in our world. There is a quality of suffering and personal sacrifice that brings about objective knowledge and understanding—itself blended with the capacity for love of mankind and love of one's neighbor—even the neighbor next to me now and here, for whom I may feel no emotional liking at all.

Here, too, every normal man or woman has experiences that show the existence of this otherwise invisible quality of feeling. A great shock, an earthquake, an accidental con-frontation with one's own moral failure, or with immense loss or the mystery of death, can bring about a radiant, however temporary, capacity of love and compassion—evidence that this capacity has been latent within the very essence of one's own human nature, but has been blanketed by the norms and mores of the external world and our childhood conditioning.

An individual has to be willing to undergo intentionally

and willingly, and usually for a considerable period of time, the kind of suffering and inner sacrifice that opens the heart in order to approach, and experience as one's own, something of the vast reaches of the unknown levels of the human mind, unknown levels of self-knowledge and knowledge of the Earth and the universal world. An ordinary "scientific attitude," sincere as it may be, can yield at best only glimpses of certain physically perceivable biological or neurological concomitants of deeper levels of consciousness.

We can hardly imagine what the Earth will offer us in return for its being seen and understood by the whole being of Man. Earth and Nature need this from us more than anything else. And only from this inner transformation of the mind can right action toward nature and the Earth be pursued without ultimately resulting in "the same old story"—that is, division, conflict and violence.

Chapter Twenty-Two

The Marriage of Fact and Meaning

E yes open, in the present moment, I picture Elias as he was—my childhood brother of the mind. We two knew nothing and cared nothing for religion or myth. We never heard of anything called spiritual tradition or inwardness. It was nature and the Earth that we knew and loved—knew and loved with the whole of ourselves.

Over the years Elias came to mind many times. What a joy it would have been to think with him about the facts and theories about the universe that he had not lived to see. How amazed he would have been, as I was, by the infinity of infinities that science is discovering in the night sky!— not only the infinity of stars, but the infinity of galaxies and clusters of galaxies, and types and shapes and colors and immensities each containing its own infinity of suns, planets and moons. Levels and levels of worlds—worlds within worlds within worlds.

And new, inconceivable entities—like the black holes, some with the mass of billions of suns, drawing into the galactic core light and space and time itself! What could such a thing *mean*? And such discoveries and theories were now arising year by year, seemingly even day by day, each time bidding fair to revolutionize our whole picture of the universe. I could almost hear Elias saying such things as: "*We* are alive—couldn't there be life always and everywhere? What if Life is the same thing as Reality?"

I remembered the silences that spread through us when we came to that kind of question—those long silences as darkness began to fall and the cold stone wall beneath us chilled us to shivering.

Those were religious silences, if the word religion has any meaning at all.

I imagined him many times over as all the sciences poured forth their torrents of discovery—from the life of and within the living cell, the astonishing communal world of bacteria, the internal, living complexity of what used to be considered merely primitive forms of life, the untangling of the structure of DNA and the replication of the genome—and I thought of the loving arguments Elias and I would have had about the interpretation of these discoveries—could the gene really be the main cause of anything in the organism? Weren't the genes themselves only the *instruments* of change and evolution? And if so, what was the real cause? Where did it reside? No matter what was being discovered, no matter what plethora of facts and suppositions and tiny details were inundating our minds, it all, everywhere, implied the existence in the universe and on the Earth of a center of meaning and purpose. Every new explanation, evolutionistic or not, only deepened the mystery.

The more light, the more mystery.

The more light, the more darkness.

The more facts, the more wonder, the more faith.

The more denials, the more assertions.

The more science, the more metaphysics.

As I imagined Elias over the years, he would have loved it all, and we together would in equal measure be both silenced and inwardly inflamed by it all.

These are all sacred stirrings of the human psyche, crying out not just for more and more discoveries, more facts and more theory, but—and this is crucial—for more consciousness, for entirely new *levels* of consciousness—although neither of us had any explicit notion of such a thing. But it was only a new consciousness that could have harmonized and conciliated the great dualities that confront every normal child and man and woman in front of what nature is revealing to us: the dualities, the contradictions between light and darkness, clarity and mystery, fact and faith, science and religion. And even in our children's minds and hearts, Elias and I—so I have come to understand with great certainty—were always moving toward the silence that appears when the mind of a human being stands *in between* great opposing truths. We were, of course, too young to realize that in that quality of silence we were standing on the threshold of a great discovery. The point is that such profound contradictions can only be reconciled *at another level of consciousness*, and not merely by means of yet another new theory or fact.

The yearning for knowledge from a higher level, the longing for the level of understanding that may be called wisdom, begins actually to be fulfilled when we willingly stand *in between* truths, between *levels* of truth. When we are silenced between light and darkness, clarity and mystery.

Which means, ultimately, in between two fundamental movements within our own being, our own inner life— between the movement outward of in-the-world discovery and the movement inward toward that higher Source calling to us from within ourselves.

It is only *in between* that we begin to live in the invisible element of feeling that can make us truly human and offer us truly human understanding. Only in between levels of ourselves do we begin to discover the meaning of the Earth and of our own life on the Earth.

Was this what lay behind the wonder and joy and humility we felt when we saw the photograph of Earth brought back to us by the Apollo 17 mission to the moon?

Was ever a fact so mythic? Was ever a photograph taken with a physical camera so like a revelation from above? Was ever the Earth so visible and invisible at one and the same time?

In that photograph, when it first appeared, fact and meaning became one. Objective fact and objective meaning became one—the former in physical space; the latter in the awareness of inner presence that is meaning itself, without words, without form.

And yet there was form, image, fact. The round Earth was alive, breathing, three dimensional—that is, the real Earth existed. The real Earth had being, was *being,* beyond all interpretation. An immense living thing huge and tiny all at once. Begging to be nursed and cared for; at the same time ancient, massive and all powerful.

The Earth was alive and we all, nearly everyone in the world, felt it as alive with a feeling that came from the unknown center of our own Earth, our own body, our own organic reality. Without so many words, we saw, at one and the same time, that we, human beings, mankind, are both of the Earth and, in that quality of seeing, beyond the Earth. And here the vast invisible reaches of space itself were sensed as symbolic icons of the pure, endless

Void, the creator-consciousness that defines Man, what the ancients called "microcosmic Man."

That photograph of the whole Earth still has this power—sometimes, sometimes when we have become a little quieter, a little more serious, a little freer from fear and desire. We can almost see her breathing, a great sentient being breathing the same air as we do, accepting the same emanations and radiations from Father Sun and His own enveloping universe of celestial worlds rotating in time measured in eons, worlds coming into being and dissolving back into the unknown Void, the fertile void that is the source of all going forth into form and manifestation and all dissolving and returning to the ancient beginning.

As the years passed, and I began to teach and write about the inner dimensions of the world's religions, I started to think of Elias in a new way—with an added dimension of poignancy, as I began to discover the depths of the primal spiritual teachings of mankind, as I began to see their visions of the Earth and the cosmos not as primitive fantasy, but as another level of truth. These visions caught my breath no less than the awesome scientific vision of nature and the universe. So much did I wish to sit down with Elias, holding in my hands some sacred book or ancient symbolic image of nature and the cosmos! *Elias*, I would say, *look at this!* Look even at our Bible—the very Bible we had always ignored or brushed aside.

Many were the scenarios I played out with Elias in my mind, often imagining him doubting and criticizing—as I had also done over the years until I began to glimpse the invisible element of real feeling. And I began to understand, through experience, why in fact it was invisible not only to me, but to all of mankind.

As I write this, I see now that Elias and I, sitting at the low stone wall, were often in touch with this invisible element of feeling when we contemplated the heavens and the Earth. But we had absolutely no idea, no conception at all—How could we? We were children—that this quality of feeling, this pure sense of wonder, was a seed of something even greater, far greater. We had no idea at all of what the sense of wonder is meant to become in us, how it is meant to develop in man. And the invisibility of this potential, after all, lies at the root of the whole human condition, the whole fate of mankind and, very possibly, of the Earth itself.

How could we know the existential price that has to be paid before the heart of man can play its necessary role in the awakening of consciousness and its power to see reality as it is in itself? We are speaking of nothing less than that. Nothing less than the capacity to know the real world, the real universe, the real Earth. And we are speaking of what is essentially unknown in our modern world and unknown in our own experience, conditioned as it is by the forces and assumptions of our culture. We are speaking of the role of feeling, an unknown, invisible level of feeling that is an indispensable component in the attainment of objective knowledge. And this element of higher, truer feeling has to be fought for, paid for in the coin of intensive inner sacrifice and struggle. It is nothing less than the struggle to become free from the domination of ego, the false sense of self that is the poisonous "gift" of our culture—not only our modern culture, but the culture of human society, stretching back in millennial time.

What may be unique in our contemporary culture is the near absence of ideas and methods of living that call us to this struggle to awaken the heart, not just for a moment of silent objective seeing—as in moments of great crisis—but as a persisting force and ideal for the whole of our lives. What we and our Mother Earth need, and what has been needed since Man first appeared, is the energy of awakened and awakening men and women. Where does this energy come from? We are told that it is within us, within the frame and structure of Man. But it is hidden.

And here we see why the countless cosmologies and visions of the Earth that have existed throughout history have always, in myth and symbol and sometimes in abstract philosophical language, placed Man and the human element deeply within the story of the universe and the Earth. From the creation stories of the Australian aboriginal Dreamtime, to the legends of the Iroquois and Navaho, to the visionary recitals of Persia and Arabia; from the book of Genesis and the mysterious immensity of the Koran and the myths within the heart of Christianity—to the hundreds of creation and cosmological legends of Africa, and the great myths and heroic tales of the Teutonic north of the world, to the Celtic dramas of cosmic struggle—and of course the thousand-faceted heart-rending, joyous and sorrowful, triumphant, and infinitely solemn ocean of stories and scriptures that comprise the vast spiritual energy of India, including the legends of the Awakened One, the Buddha, also in company of cosmic gods and goddesses—the Awakened One especially under his names of *Dharmakaya, Sambhogakaya* and *Nirmanakhaya*, indicating, among other things, nothing less than enlightened consciousness as the essence of the universe itself, compassion as the essence of cosmic space.

Man, human man, container of unfathomed reaches of sensation, thought and feeling, is the reality of reality itself, is implicated in everything from electron to galactic cluster. Not the puny being we are, living and dying on the surface of our internal universal being. Not that puny being dreaming egoistic fantasies and suffering egoistic emotions. But Man above and within us, calling out to us to be let into our lives and to nourish the Earth and complete the work of Sun-infused nature that is our temporary home.

Look up at the stars—so the thousands of primal creation myths tell us—look up at the sky, look around you at the immeasurable kaleidoscope of nature and nature's laws, look through the great lenses of our own astonishing technologies, down to the level of subatomic waves—what do we see? God? Perhaps we can call it that. But also Man. We see ourselves—or, rather, we see reality calling to us to know what we are and what we are meant to be: consciousness that creates, loves, wills and acts in accordance with the highest truths of the universal world.

The human element is at the heart of all the cosmologies and creation myths of mankind—symbolically and explicitly. Which means the element of feeling and struggle and purpose—the struggle between love and anger, light and gravity, hunger and joy, genius and foolishness, tenderness and lust, jealousy and sacrifice, pride and remorse. All this is involved in the universe as much as, and in a sense, more than, the levels of astronomical worlds we perceive in outer space.

Look through our great telescopes: Do you see Man? No, of course not. You see chemical reactions, physical laws, explosions, mergings, seemingly violent births and deaths. You, we, do not see Man because it is not Man who is looking through the telescope. It is only part of man: The isolated rational mind, with all its undeniable brilliance, is only a small part of man, of the human psyche.

But if the whole man, if a whole man with all his faculties of perception looks through that same telescope, he will see himself, what he truly is. He will see what the ancient sages and tellers of myth saw in nature, in the Earth, above the Earth, in the sky. He, we, will see passion and truth and love and yearning and the needs of God and the Earth themselves.

We do not see Man in the universe because it is not Man who is looking. Look with the eyes of true Man and you, we, will see true Man in all his cosmic drama and cosmic duty to himself, the Earth and Sun and beyond.

All this I would have wished to speak about with my childhood friend.

In fact, it somehow seems to me that now, here, in this very moment, I *am* speaking to him.

Chapter Twenty-Three

Invisible Earth

We need to understand that the ancient cosmologies and creation myths were not simply about the human dimension in the universe and in the meaning of the Earth. These tales are not simply telling us about the hidden element of higher feeling, especially in their hero tales and in the stories of struggles among the gods of heaven and the demons of hell. Something much more fundamental must be understood in referring to these ancient visions. We need to consider that *in their original and authentic form*, these cosmological teachings and mythologies not only contained teachings *about* the hidden element of higher feeling, but these teachings and myths themselves were at their genuine origin *created* by the action in the mind of this hidden element. That is to say, the ancient cosmologies were products of men and women of a higher level of being. And often enough the symbols and stories speak of the nature of the extraordinary struggle that must be undergone in order to open the heart of the seeker to this hidden element that brings with it knowledge and understanding of another level than what we know as objective knowledge. Not only do these myths speak about the attainment of consciousness, they are the product of it—and contain keys to the kind of inner struggle necessary for its attainment.[29]

Having said this much, we may also add that this kind of knowledge is contained not only in story and doctrine, but it involves and can involve all of what we may call the conscious service of art—including music, dance, and visual representations—ritual, methods of meditation and prayer, and the indispensable inner work of opening to the conscious sensation of the body.

But most of all, these representations of the unknown struggle for conscious feeling and truly objective knowledge are meant to indicate and support an entirely new and eternally unknown relationship between man and man. This ever-new and eternally needed struggle involves nothing less than the practice of sacrificing our deep, unfathomably deep, identification with the egoism that over the millennia has become embedded in our nature. The inner work required as preparation for this sacrifice requires extraordinary help and the knowledge of what it really means to work on oneself. This is the reason for carefully protected monasteries and authentic spiritual communities.

There is an egoism, a self-love, that is easily recognized within ourselves, and there is a struggle with this egoism that is called for by the moral teachings that originally entered our culture, sometimes from very deep sources— but which is also called for by enlightened and inspired men and women who draw their understanding solely from human reasoning and human sensibilities. These are the moralities and the ideals which many of us try to live by. But these are also the moralities that perhaps all of us, if we are sincere, now begin to recognize as ultimately powerless to rescue our lives and our Earth from the brink of devastation. Could this be because there is a deeper egoism within us that is actually unknown to us, and which is untouched by our usual moral struggles? Could it even be that sometimes, not always, but often, *our conventional morality actually screens the deeper egoism within us?*— by making us imagine that we are capable of doing what only a conscious man is able to do: to love, to be impartial, to will.

And could it therefore be that there is a deeper struggle with ourselves, our deeper egoism, that is as unknown as the invisible forces that shape the universe itself?

Earth, is this finally what you need from your children

of the Sun? Because what lies on the other side of that unknown struggle is, and has always been, the true human being always waiting to be born, the unknown world called Man. And the unknown capacity yearning to emerge from behind the depths of our essence-egoism can now be given its proper name, cleansed of all its centuries-old accretions and crusts: Love.

A new definition of Man: Man is the being who is able to love—who, with the mind cleansed by love, can know reality as it is in itself. Who can then *do* all that for which he has been created.

Chapter Twenty-Four

The Unfinished Animal

I am back at the low stone wall.

In the dream it is just before dawn. For hours throughout the night, under a black sky, I have been waiting for Elias. In the dream, I remember once again the last word I heard him say to me as we were climbing the forested hill along the Wissahickon Creek. I had just "seen" inside the mind of the doubly young and old Elias: an infinitely deep sky full of blazing stars, an endless universe behind his forehead, inside the very head upon his shoulders. I nearly fell to my knees.

Then and there I believed that, sensing my astonishment, he was just about to speak about what I had seen, but the sound of the wind and the rushing water of the Wissahickon, the sounds of the Earth, had drowned out his voice—it seemed he was saying something about the true uniqueness of man.

But when I had asked him to repeat what he said, he answered with only one word: *later*.

Now, in the dream, at the low stone wall, as dark night begins to give way to pale daylight, I see not one, but two shadowy figures approaching—a man and a boy. It is soon clear that the man is Elias, but I cannot make out the identity of the boy whose hand Elias is holding. Even when they are quite close I still cannot see who the boy is. My emotion tells me that the boy is me, but in my dream-consciousness I cannot clearly see the features of his face.

Elias appears as I have never seen him before in these dreams. His face is both more concentrated and deeply serene. Gone is the sorrow and the grief that had been there so much before. The wrinkled brow is now as wondrously smooth as it was when he was young, and the lines in his face are as strong and profound as the chiseled lines of a stone statue.

Instead of sitting next to me on the wall, he and the boy sit down on the ground, facing me. Elias gently draws the boy closer toward him until they are touching and then with his other hand reaches across and lightly touches the boy's hair with his fingertips. His wrist loosely relaxed, he holds his left hand there, just above the boy's head.

Benevolently looking down at the boy, who is still facing

me, but whose features I still cannot make out, Elias begins to speak, but no sound reaches me. As this is going on, a few small birds fly down to the ground behind Elias and stand there just looking on. They make some bird sounds, which I can hear quite clearly, even though I cannot hear anything of what Elias is saying.

Elias is not looking at me; he is looking down at the earth. Gradually, the boy's full face begins to become visible—as though emerging out of a thin mist. I recognize him immediately as myself as I was when Elias and I first started meeting so many years ago there at the low stone wall.

But what is Elias saying? I still cannot hear him. His left hand remains poised just above the boy's head, *my* head.

Surprising myself, I whisper to myself, under my breath, "Be still. Study."

Trying somehow to follow my own inner command, I find myself awake and asleep at the same time, fully aware of myself lying in bed, my head on the pillow, and yet also deeply immersed in the dream. In that dual state of consciousness I stand back from myself in the dream and I see arising in me another kind of feeling, enormously strong. A sense of wonder and joy, together with a heartbreaking feeling of remorse for my life. Inexplicable.

While all this is happening, seemingly over a long period of time, I notice that a forest of trees has appeared there in the neighborhood of our low stone wall—trees where in reality there used to be nothing but row houses and cracked cement sidewalks lining a narrow, tar-covered street covering the Earth.

At the same time, I am aware that many kinds of birds are appearing in the forest of trees surrounding me: sparrows, crows, robins, parrots, even an eagle from some far-off place. I hear them, but I still cannot hear Elias.

"Elias!" I call out. "Tell me what is happening! Please!"

Elias remains still, soundlessly speaking, his left hand unmovingly poised just above the head of my twelve-year-old self whose eyes are now closed.

Many more birds, large and small, are flying down from the sky, settling in the trees, all sounding their calls in a growing, somehow harmonious din. Out of the corner of my eye, I notice animals beginning to emerge from beneath the trees.

After the passage of who knows how long a time, my twelve-year-old eyes open and then close again and his, *my*, lips ever so slightly curve into a tranquil smile.

With that I wake up, sensing that this will be the last dream of Elias that I will have.

IT IS MUCH later in the morning. Working at my desk, while absently watching some squirrels flying through the thick cluster of trees outside my window, I notice with a start an oblong, Styrofoam-backed poster that for years I have had propped up against the windowpane. It is the photograph of a small statue above the north porch of Chartres Cathedral outside Paris. Upon the curved arch of the cathedral entrance—an arch that resembles the high-arched bridge that appeared as I climbed above the Wissahickon with Elias—there are numerous carvings of animals and plants representing the creation of life and the world, the creation of the Earth. Amid all these small, exquisite representations of nature, almost hidden among them, there are two carvings depicting the creation of Adam, the creation of Man. The one that for years has been in my field of vision every morning shows Adam at God's knee, his head tenderly resting in God's hands. Here God is not the overwhelming, majestic ancient as in so much of Christian art. Here he is a strong and gentle mature human figure, his own head bent in loving regard for the being that he is bringing to life.

Here the hands of God precisely mirror the hands of the grown Elias in the dream. As in the dream, the fingertips of the relaxed left hand of God are all but touching the top of Adam's head—an image, as I now see it, representing the infusion of the transforming energy from above that can descend into and through the body of a human being in the process of deep awakening.

As for Adam's serene smile in the carving, it is exactly my own in the dream.

There cannot be many traditional portrayals of this iconic event that so touchingly show the creation of Man to be an act of love, and that show the joy that Man is born to in his essential nature.

This image is astonishing. But what to me is also astonishing is that, having been directly in front of this image almost every day for more than five years, it is only just now in this moment that I become aware of one of the most vital and vivid elements in it, one that has been staring me in the face without my seeing it. For all these years I've wondered why we are shown only the upper body of Adam as he bends his head at God's knee. I vaguely attributed it to the odd-looking folds of God's robe covering him, or to some of the statue having broken away during the passage of time. And I made nothing more of it.

Yet now, it is clear and obvious that in this image Adam is only half emerged from the dust of the Earth.

Man is incomplete, unfinished. None of the animals carved in stone along the cathedral arch are depicted in this way. Here man, uniquely among the creatures of Earth, is, in Gurdjieff's words, the "unfinished animal." In him, the process of evolution on the Earth cannot proceed automatically in the way it is usually imagined by modern science or by various philosophies and theologies influenced by science. The next stage in the evolution of life on the Earth depends on the intentional inward effort of man. Without this effort, this unique inner struggle, this unique movement of inwardness and its outer manifestation in willed action, the growth of the tree of life on Earth may come to a stop. If humanity becomes unable to awaken to what the Earth needs from it, the life of the Earth itself may come to an end. The future growth of the Earth, according to this teaching, depends on the reception by the Earth of a conscious energy that only man is capable of transmitting. That is why we are here in an unimaginably complex, unfinished body built joyously to receive and obey this conscious energy "from above." This is the energy of an ever-new consciousness, the energy of evolving life at this centuries-long moment of Earth's history. It is not the energy of merely mental knowledge, which by itself almost inevitably serves the formation of our unnatural egoism. In this sense, the tree of life profoundly stands apart from the tree of the knowledge of good and evil.

Not far from the *Creation of Adam*, equally small, equally difficult to notice even when seen from right below the arch, is a carving in which the same image of God is presented now seated and looking out upon his as yet incomplete creation of the world. But who is that clear, smooth youthful figure standing just behind him, looking out from behind God's shoulder?

In my hands I am holding a postcard photograph of this second carving. Turning it over, I am once again stopped by the explanation furnished on the back of this modest tourist memento—an explanation, offered by who knows what authority, and with who knows what evidence:

God conceives the idea of Man while observing the flight of the birds.

Why does this explanation thrill me?

Why does it so deeply touch me?

Why are we here, what forces have brought Man to the Earth?

And what *is* Man? Can we say that we are that specific two-natured being, like none other on Earth, meant to live both fully engaged in the forces of human life on Earth and fully engaged in keen obedience to that undiscovered immortal energy within ourselves which we are called to offer to the groaning world that is our Earth? Can we say that we are that being, Man, like no other being on this planet, created to stand in between these two directions of inner and outer consciousness—and in that place in between to discover our own real identity, our own real name?

Do we know this? Have we heard this name called? In fact, it is a name written into our essence, a name continu-ously given to us, not only long ago on a holy mountain, and not only in the utterances and songs and spaces of the

East, but now and here, in this moment—could we but remember our selves, could we but remember our name: *I Am*.

Could we understand science as the main form of our modern era's movement outward into nature and the created world? Then how to move inward, without fantasy or despair, toward the unknown world within? What guidance, what help, is necessary? Perhaps we will discover that it is only standing in between these two movements, caring attentively, passionately for each, that we will be given the moral power to care for the living Earth.

Notes

1. Vernadsky, Vladimir. *The Biosphere*. 1986, p. 8. See Book Notes for further bibliographic information. "The biosphere is as much, or even more, the creation of the Sun as it is a manifestation of Earth-processes. Ancient religious intuitions which regarded terrestrial creatures, especially human beings, as 'children of the Sun' were much nearer the truth than those which looked upon them as a mere ephemeral creation, a blind and accidental product of matter and earth-forces."

2. Vernadsky. See Book Notes.

3. Taittiriya Upanishad: 2.9.1.

4. Lovelock, James. *Gaia: A New Look at Life on Earth*. Oxford: Oxford University Press, 2000. Also by Lovelock: *The Vanishing Face of Gaia: A Final Warning*. New York: Basic Books, 2009.

5. McKibben, Bill. *The End of Nature*. New York: Random House, 1989. McKibben's devastating analysis, *Eaarth*, had not yet appeared at that time.

6. Easterbrook, Gregg. *A Moment on the Earth*. New York: Viking Penguin, 1995.

7. Berry, Thomas. *The Great Work: Our Way into the Future*. New York: Bell Tower, 1999.

8. Abram, David. *The Spell of the Sensuous: Perception and Language in a More-Than-Human World*. New York: Random House, 1996.

9. Murchie, Guy. *The Seven Mysteries of Life*. Boston: Houghton Mifflin, 1978.

10. See Book Notes.

11. Corbin, Henry. "Eyes of Flesh and Eyes of Fire: Science and Gnosis." In *Material for Thought*, Vol. 8. San Francisco: Far West Institute. This brief but telling essay can be read online at www.farwesteditions.com.

12. Praśna Upanishad: First Praśna 9, 10.

13. Genesis 1:28 (King James Version).

14. Binswanger, Ludwig. "Freud and the Magna Carta of Clinical Psychiatry." In *Being in the World: Selected Papers of Ludwig Binswanger*, translated and edited by Jacob Needleman. New York: Basic Books, 1963, p. 182.

15. Descartes, René. *Meditations on First Philosophy*.

16. Kierkegaard, Søren. *Fear and Trembling*. Translated by Walter Lowrie. Princeton, N.J.: Princeton University Press, 1941.

17. Kierkegaard. *Concluding Unscientific Postscript*. Trans-

lated by David F. Swenson and Walter Lowrie. Princeton, N.J.: Princeton University Press, 1941.

18. *The Sickness Unto Death,* p. 17. See Book Notes.

19. See Book Notes.

20. See Book Notes.

21. *The Sickness Unto Death,* p. 19.

22. Langmuir, Charles H., and Wally Broecker. *How to Build a Habitable Planet: The Story of Earth from the Big Bang to Humankind,* revised and expanded edition. Princeton, N.J.: Princeton University Press, 2012, Chapter 17, p. 536 (emphasis added). See Book Notes.

23. Needleman, Jacob. *A Sense of the Cosmos: Scientific Knowledge and Spiritual Truth.* Rhinebeck, New York: Monkfish Book Publishing Company, 2003, pp. 44–45.

24. Jeans, James. *The Mysterious Universe.* New York: Macmillan, 1933, p. 186.

25. Russell, Bertrand. "A Free Man's Worship." In *Why I Am Not a Christian.* New York: Allen and Unwin, 1957, pp. 105–116.

26. For further reading suggestions about Plato, see Book Notes.

27. One of the very few potent and lucid explications of *Timaeus* may be found embedded in *Living Time* by Maurice Nicoll (Eureka Editions and out-of-print sources). Overall, *Living Time* is an extraordinary blending of cosmology, metaphysics and spiritual psychology.

28. Werblowsky, R. J. Zwi. "Judaism, or the Religion of Israel." In *The Concise Encyclopedia of Living Faiths,* edited by R. C. Zaehner. Boston: Beacon Press, 1959, p. 29.

29. Here I would like to refer the reader to two examples from my own books where I have tried to indicate the symbolic power of such legends and myths. One example is the Iroquois legend of the formation of its governing constitution, as depicted in *The American Soul* (New York: Tarcher/Penguin, 2001). A second is the myth of King Solomon and his exile as told in *Money and the Meaning of Life* (New York: Doubleday, 1991). See also the Kabbalistic myth of Creation in *Major Trends in Jewish Mysticism* by Gershom Scholem (New York: Schocken Books, 1961).

Book Notes

Vladimir I. Vernadsky (1863–1947), *The Biosphere.* First published in 1926. The excerpt cited in Chapter Four of the present book is from the opening pages of a working translation from the French and Russian completed under the direction of Dr. David B. Langmuir in San Francisco and Los Angeles in 1977. That excerpt and further excerpts from that particular translation were published in the journal *Material for Thought,* San Francisco, Far West Editions, 1977, vol. 7, pp. 27–37 (www.farwesteditions.com). A revised and annotated edition of the Langmuir translation, done under the direction of Mark A. S. McMenamin, with a foreword by Lynn Margulis, was published as *The Biosphere* in 1998 under the Nevraumont/Copernicus imprint of Springer-Verlag, New York. The annotations offer extensive and illuminating observations of Vernadsky's insights in relation to more recent scientific research. The first published English translation of *The Biosphere* was an abridgment published in London in 1986 by Synergetic Press, now located in Santa Fe, New Mexico. This translation, unabridged and coupled with other major writings of Vernadsky, was published by Synergetic Press in 2007 under the title *Geochemistry and the Biosphere,* edited by Frank B. Salisbury and translated by Olga Barash.

All of the above translations communicate a sense of the genius that Vernadsky brings to the study of the Earth: the heart of a visionary philosopher combined with the intellect of a pioneering scientific observer and theoretician who provided many of the basic tools for ecology as a science. From our point of view, his most important contribution is the extent to which he shows that it is life that shapes the Earth, not the other way around. Living things construct the environment— it has always been so. Thus the question of the present book: With the appearance of Man, what is the necessary role of purely human consciousness *as such* in the further evolution of our Earth?

Søren Kierkegaard (1813–1855), *The Sickness Unto Death* (Princeton, N.J.: Princeton University Press, 1941) and *The Concept of Dread* (Princeton University Press, 1944), both translated by Walter Lowrie. Be warned. Except for occasional brief, blazing, lightning flashes of psychological and spiritual insight, and breathtaking wit, almost all of Kierkegaard's uniquely profound writings are more or less inaccessible without preparation and guidance, even though, simply as a writer, he has few equals. That said, I in good conscience strongly recommend his books. In them any one of us can experience the shock of truth.

One of the best books to prepare most readers is the carefully chosen compilation of excerpts from his journals: *The Diary of Søren Kierkegaard*, edited by Peter Rohde (New York: Citadel Press, 1998).

Charles H. Langmuir and Wally Broecker, *How to Build a Habitable Planet: The Story of Earth from the Big Bang to Humankind,* revised and expanded edition (Princeton, N.J.: Princeton University Press, 2012). Drawing on all the major disciplines of physical science, this sweeping account tells Earth's complete story as science sees it—from the unfathomable origin and immensities of the universe and the starry world to the equally unfathomable minuteness of the subnuclear world, ultimately focusing on the role of human civilization in the life of our planet. The book concludes by contemplating how to keep our Earth habitable and even, perhaps, participate in its further evolution. Intended as an introductory college text, it is written with a clarity that anyone, even with relatively little scientific background, can appreciate. The result is the outline of an undeniably dramatic, nearly mythic story that is greater than the sum of its parts. Even with all its impeccable scientific detail, this book can lead the reader to the literary equivalent of standing on the Earth, looking up at a sky full of shining worlds, while at the same time asking oneself the ancient questions: What is Man? What am I?

P. D. Ouspensky (1878–1947), *In Search of the Miraculous* (New York: Harcourt, Brace and Company, 1949). In 1912, G. I. Gurdjieff appeared in Moscow "out of nowhere," a man seemingly unlike anyone else in the world. The strength of his human presence, the startling newness and depth of his insight about man and the universe, and his subtle and demanding manner of spiritual guidance attracted a small circle of pupils drawn largely from the Russian intelligentsia. One of these pupils, in 1915, in St. Petersburg, was the spiritual philosopher P. D. Ouspensky, whose book *Tertium Organum* had established him as a leading writer on mystical and esoteric questions. For the next several years, in the midst of the long earthquake of the Russian Revolution, Gurdjieff poured out his teaching about the meaning of human life on Earth, encompassing what he later characterized as "all and everything"—cosmology, science, religious tradition, the psychology of consciousness, art, the world of nature and, above all, the grim future of "sleeping" humanity, together with masterful practical indications of the hope to be found through the inner work toward awakening.

In Search of the Miraculous is Ouspensky's artful and elec-
trifying record of these years and the teaching he received.
Paraphrasing the words of one observer [Michel de Salzmann,
"Footnote to the Gurdjieff Literature" in *Gurdjieff: An Annotated Bibliography* by J. Walter Driscoll and The Gurdjieff
Foundation of California (New York: Garland Publishing,
Inc., 1985), p. xviii], the secret quality emanating from this
book comes precisely from the fact that it takes us as closely as
possible to the conditions of what has been called "the oral
tradition," in which the force of the teacher's presence brings
about an "incarnation" of the ideas, enabling pupils to open to
entirely new dimensions of thought and feeling within themselves. This book remains, in my opinion, the best introduc-
tion to the Gurdjieff teaching.

Henry Corbin (1903–1978), *Spiritual Body and Celestial Earth*
(Princeton, N.J.: Princeton University Press, 1977). Henry
Corbin, French philosopher and theologian, was one of the
twentieth century's greatest scholars of religion, though it
would be more accurate to speak of him, echoing what has
been said of Vernadsky, as a master of visionary scholarship.
In his profound studies of Islamic, especially Persian, mystical
recitations, he identified what he called the "imaginal world"—
the Earth as perceived in higher states of consciousness. The

haunting title of the book is a clue to the meaning of the *imaginal:* the intermediate world paradoxically blending and bridging the world perceived by the senses and the Godly world that transcends the senses. The imaginal is the world of meanings, rather than facts and logic alone. Describing the writings of one of the great Persian mystics, Corbin says: "The Earth he speaks of is not the same as the one which supports our feet, and is now being devastated by the ambitions of our reckless conquests. It is the 'Earth of Light,' which one can only perceive with the eyes of the heart. But it is up to us, to each one of us, to regard this Earth with eyes that are capable of seeing it . . . so that it (may) reveal to us our own secrets, whose existence we barely suspect."

This book, like so many of Corbin's studies, is a jewel-studded forest of ideas and imagery, much of which may remain obscure to the reader, but which can yield an unforgettable overall impression of the "invisible Earth" that is calling for our deepest attention and love.

Gustav Theodor Fechner (1801–1887). Widely considered the father of experimental psychology, Gustav Fechner combined a brilliant scientific intellect with the mind of what can best be called a mystical empiricist. The full summary of his vision of the Earth as a life form of a higher order than man can be found in William James's *A Pluralistic Universe* in Chapter IV,

"Concerning Fechner." I urge anyone who is interested in the questions treated in this book to read it. An excellent collection of Fechner's writings exists under the title *Religion of a Scientist* (New York: Pantheon Books, 1946), edited and translated by Walter Lowrie (also the translator of Kierkegaard).

In the opening pages of his *Spiritual Body and Celestial Earth,* Henry Corbin states how inspired he was by a passage in Fechner's essay "Concerning Souls," where Fechner tells "how on a spring morning, while a transfiguring light cast a halo over the face of the earth, he [Fechner] was struck not merely by the esthetic idea, but by the vision and the concrete evidence that the Earth is an Angel"—so much so that he "wondered how men's notions could be so perverted as to see in the Earth only a dry clod. . . ."

Stephan Harding (1953–), *Animate Earth: Science, Intuition, and Gaia* (Totnes, Devon, England: Green Books, Ltd., 2006). "Our world," Stephan Harding writes, "is in crisis, and, regrettably, our way of doing science in the West has inadvertently contributed to the many problems we face." Inspired by James Lovelock's concept of Gaia, the author, who holds a doctorate in ecology from Oxford University, offers a scientifically grounded vision of Earth considered as a living, animate being with needs, purposes, wisdom and struggles of her own. I have been much helped by his effort to complement the objectifying attitude of science with the warmth and respect owed to a living being with a soul.

Plato (424/423 BCE –348/347 BCE). There exist many translations of the works of Plato that exhibit high levels of scholarship. In my opinion, the widely known renditions by the nineteenth-century scholar Benjamin Jowett still communicate an unsurpassed sense of the grandeur of the enterprise of philosophy itself as well as the profundity and subtlety of great philosophical thought. A remarkable and clearly written guide to Plato's vast vision of both the ethical and the cosmic meaning of human life is *Therapeia* by Robert Cushman (New Brunswick, N.J.: Transaction Publishers, 2002).

Index

evolution
 Earth's dependence upon man,
  135–38
 intentions of Earth, 133
 levels of chance in, 111–12
 of man within evolution of
  Earth, 109–10
 movement toward unity,
  111, 117
 outer and inner evolution,
  132–33
 scientific view of, 130–32
 third force of life, 153
 through intentional inward
  effort of man, 195

Fechner, Gustav, 98–99
feeling and emotion
 authentic feeling, free of
  egoism, 170–71
 as egoism, 168
 influence on perception and
  thought, 168
 invisible element in knowledge
  and consciousness,
  166–67, 177, 181
 struggle and inner sacrifice,
  172–73, 183, 186–88
flat earth, 125

Gaia concept, 53, 97
God
 as connection to universe, 18
 creation of unfinished man, 194
 divine aspects of human
  consciousness, 100–101

harmonization of realities of
  mind and nature,
  64–65, 72
 inner and outer meaning in
  language of, 33–35
 love in creation of man, 194
 man's dependence upon, 102,
  110
 reality immersed in purposes
  of, 146–48
 scientific objectivity
  concerning, 34–35,
  110–11
 synthesis of Heaven and Earth
  within man, 64, 94, 101,
  106, 120
 third force of life, 66, 72
Great Work, The (Berry), 54
Gurdjieff, G. I.
 on awakened man, 136,
  152–53, 157
 on purpose of life on earth, 25,
  134–36
 teachings for Earth and
  universe, 158–59

Hegel, Georg, 73
Hinduism, 149, 161
hope engendered by truth,
  159–60
How to Build a Habitable Planet
  (Langmuir), 104, 108–9

I Am, 29, 197
Indian sacred teachings
 Awakened One, 182